DIASPORA

DIASPORA

Amadou B.H. Sey

To order additional copies of this book, contact:
Xlibris Corporation
0-800-644-6988
www.xlibrispublishing.co.uk
Orders@xlibrispublishing.co.uk
303679

CONTENTS

DEDICATION

First and foremost, thanks and praises to the almighty God. Thanks to my late parents who sacrificed a lot and gave me the opportunity to be literate. Not forgetting my loving and lovely wife and children, without their cooperation and encouragement, this book of poems might not have been written.

I also remember my co-workers, friends, brothers and sisters living in West Africa, EU, and the USA. My acknowledgement also goes to my memorable teachers and lecturers, from primary to university level. I am honouring also my best friends and colleagues, both remote and immediate. Thanks also to my readers. With you I shall exist, and without you I would be null and void. Thanking also The Xlibris Publishing Company for making this book available to all.

Finally, my heartfelt compliments and support to freedom and democracy.

Amadou bh Sey

MIGRATION OF THE HELPLESS

In desolation and disarray
Belongings gathered in the blazing sun
Although cold as ice in the climax of war
In some lands
Mass migration, into no-man's-land in the tropics too

No chance to allow babies to suckle
For their parents' shoes on buckle at departure
Thus day ride on the back of dust-ridden thorns
Limping along, their feet rot in rust.

Running away from torture of open enemies
Labour camps rampant and their gates wide open
Some weak and powerless, although migrants
In no-man's-land, law of the jungle thrives
Scrambling over any piece of food made available,
But no spare time to cook badly needed meals.

Fast food meals mulch in haste
Hating is no crime in this condition
Struggling hard to safety
Those involved are helpless marauders
Breathless and restless are the migrants.

26 May 93-Sunday, 01 July 2007

ON THE BRINK "TRIBUTE TO ALL ARMY OFFICERS FALLEN OR ALIVE"

Was half, now at brim?
As was strong now at brink
Little hope to survive the weight
The brink of brake of death

Soldiers are human too
Not iron men or robots
Called upon in times of crises
And discarded forgotten in peace and joy
When cowards hide beneath blankets

Listen to the commander that commands commanders
All to kill or capture
Or be killed
For they have been trained so
Or defend their lands
Not the objective of the soldier though
Put aside international law
It is human law and life that matters now

Beware that soldiers are mothered too
And they do love and marry, thus are fathers too
Now at brink in this century they stand
In strings of patients so tight

Any further pull renders rapture
Putting our nations,
At their mercy as they retaliate.
Rectifying errors of human history
Within risk a final collapse
Of what we use to call state security

26 May 1993-Sunday, 01 July 2007

A VICTIM OF THE SYSTEM

How can we change the trend of global crises?
For this issue is a global theme
Unprecedented arrests!
Little explanations allowed, to rest
Handcuffs talk and the soles of boots trample in test.

The warrant to arrest the innocent
Satisfying the ball-heads' nonsense
If I hate him, you have to lament
Questions aren't necessary
Go ahead and do the robots job variety.

For thinking makes you human, your ego
Local slogans in the old days ago
Sergeant said you go
Meaning you come with us
You are under arrest
In subdue you are done
And denying the order dooms you to pieces, on the floor
All, as clubs fall on you, as they interrogate
To accept by hook or by crook
Or get broken
For if not, they and their bus in heat
Never be at ease to cheat.

26 May 93-Sunday, 01 July 2007

THE REBEL

Why does he exist?
Is it social injustice?
Is it political influence?
Most likely a social instability
Is it economic strain or in equality?
What could be the cause?
Hunger and starvation
Yes! The thirst for liberation from tyranny

Day in day out, revolts, he the rebel, scampers
Express vice and virtue ignorant obvious
Assured in rage to retaliate dictatorship
Evading corruption and fascism, wrong for right

How can you negotiate, Mr Rebel, armed?
Ready to fire your enemy outright
Rebel! Stop and think in the end you may govern but
Damaged brains and heaps of ashes in ruins
Created by the bombs and bullets you fired

Are they also rebels or devils?
Terrorists in high jacks
What of outcasts in ghettos?
Avoid hatred rebels
Vice may thrive but temporary
Anger ends in remorse and regret
Though, hard to be patient,
Beneath mountains of wrong.

27 May 1993-Sunday, 01 July 2007

THE TRIGGER HAPPY GUYS MADLY FIRING!

Call me hazardous
Miner but destructive when touch and pulled, backwards trust
Warn the human finger that disturbs my sleep
Must do my duty if assigned to
Was I animate, surely must be rigid.

Just to kill if ever I do not get rigid
Aimed to abolish existence in assassinations
Execution annihilates humanity I preach
Then alternative to rest
Can't go on killing
I therefore revolt.

In to be used, ready I am, not against your brother
Mark I am inanimate
Therefore can't reason good and bad
Use me to celebrate.
Above and in the air
Through it I send my child
The bullet is my child, delivered to go far
Into human flesh, I burrow deep down
In most cases destroy when I land on deadly points.

My destination is thus reserved
Until sent by the human finger
By those who live amongst you as human but devils
So innocent I hang bellow.

27 May 93-Sunday, 01 July 2007

THE UNAVOIDABLE

So many samples at hand
Day to day examples
No force to deviate the course
The course of river current waves
The trend of the wind, blowing and sometimes disturbing!
Destructive hurricane winds whirl.

What is to be must be
No matter what we wish
Then why worry each other?
So no need for jealousy!
What's in possession is what is!

That should not make you dorsal mark you
For their exists arithmetic
As two and two equals to four!
But something else when tempered with
Diverted by human vice

An accident is only that!
Remain united and avoid scepticism
All answers are with Him
The Supreme Being of all worlds
Whose formulae are always correct!
Perfectly computed to suit time and space
For only we could see indeed!

17 May 1993-Thursday, 05 July 2007

COLONIES

Get together rampant in secretive hidden dungeons
Aims associated to keep united
Stay together and think together!
Become one, execute objectives, and remain so!

Games succeed in them
Societies exist and function amicably
Religious pilgrims in the inertia of progress are prone
Clubs, societies, indeed essential

Not to play only indoors such as draft
Not only to hide and smoke opium in closed doors
Get into even ghettos and discuss ideas!
Beneficial to the progress of human kinds breed!
Bridges of generations!
From creations, essential societies bred truth.

Truth! The premier and the last!
For without sin all have been born
Grow thus into clubs and conferences
Where ideas prop up in wonders
Innovations and initiatives on tables
Come together in companies
Never miniaturize others' thoughts!

27 May 1993-Thursday, 05 July 2007

CONSULTATION IN CREATING MUTUAL RELATIONS

Embark on constant consolation and consultations
Console the savages in rage
Pride promotes ignorance in this notion
Never feel fat to enquire information

Feel no fear inferiority complex
To call the savages' attention
No matter how they react
Being in wild rage, no ears to hear!
No mind to understand suggestions of compromise
Deep down in a casket of who cares!
Thus how can you be concerned?

To reconcile be sure to console both functions
Consolidate in solidarity, then freedom thrives
Avoid selfish diversion and unite
Obedient souls are always victorious
Doomed in this era, are those who do not reason
Reasoning always is the key.

So here I plea for your attention
As I always did
With all conscience open
Never feel too big and proud
For human society needs progress
Never mind changing in retrogress.

31 May 1993-Thursday, 05 July 2007

WHAT ELSE?

The objective to have it, looking up into the night sky
As I thought that to wish, to acquire this aim at my will
What is the next aim? The unknown result inspiration
My wish in aim and my destiny at my will
In conflict and confusion these are woven

Can it be obtained but by what means, in bare hands?
My instinct in faith, in future, a saint I wish to be!
Isolated worship in that mosque or is it a temple
So what else? I asked in satisfaction if in worship
This is the picture that alternates, stained in my hand!

In wish at the climax of success or loss in grief
The apex of my patience, my efforts of mind and body
Could I go on to such in gloom, a soul imprisoned?
Going round and round within and still in question
Mistaken I may be in my destination, I am confident
Having faith in ALLAH, who surely is the all knower

My path disguised, in my wish, in a dream, in green!
Come close my saviour at all moments of captivity
My mind in lust, having lost all but not you, oh Allah!
For you come always in the best of times
With the power of patience, I plead
No alternation but submission to my hope.
The hope for my rescue, now exhausted
For now is the time
To achieve that wish still in suspense!

31 May 1993-23 July 2007

THE DENIAL

Victims follow up helplessly crying
Craving crazily to get at it, trying!
The denied are pleading to the human race
Love manipulation at stake!
When the ignorant, bold, stupid are in control

So safety for those fellows as passengers
Those denied enjoying mutual or mother love
Hear that internal cry in their hearts!
Those in love in this constant wicked denial
Where race, colour, and status matters zero!
The faithfulness of lovers at risk of divorce
Endangered to sink down into the depth of that pool

The pool of jealousy in storm
Wrecking or attempting to wreck good links
Of society and the globe at large
The hopes at the brink of shock
In separation no hope to see once more
The hangover to the denial of their right
Triggering violent reactions and disorder in chaos
For in their realization they refuse
To accept unfair negotiations
Leading to further chaos!

3 June 1993-23 July 2007

DELICIOUS SACRIFICE TOBASKI

Annually, worship for the faithful in joy and laughter
It's a sacrifice as teachings and preachers say
Some indeed overdo and therefore exceed
On this day animals, in calibres are solemnly slaughtered!
Facing east in the direction of the KAABA
Towards the holy mosque in Mecca we always bow!
That great block and holy black nucleus
Now wrong used as an excuse to slaughter innocent souls!
Look at the human sacrifice rampant all over the world.

Take the ram from heaven in the order of Allah!
As the angel Gabriel flew in a semi-spiral
The noblest ram was submitted I suppose
Substituting and saving Islam's heroes
Whose name is Ismail and Abraham?
The father was faithfully relieved
So why not also those being slaughtered now!
Frequently so often we witness these horrible scenes of terror!

Intimately moved were both father and son
Thus as submitting to the will of Allah! Move on then!
History revealed and unveiled in generations
As worship with sacrifice continues on and on
Strengthening the day in joy and laughter
Amidst delicious diets in holy dishes
Meat in abundance passed to the poor and needy
Family and neighbour visits in robes
The order of this day is all joy in worship
So stop killing humans in the name of Allah
What a mountainous sin!

3 June 1993-23 July 2007

WHAT IS NOT YOURS! HONESTY

It is not yours, so why are you greedy pal?
Take not; it is not your property!
Why accepting your wants dominate
Or control your subconscious mind?
And the movement of your arms to pick up pockets
Oh Thief! Is this dissatisfaction or greed?
The need to own what you never earned
This is no pride
Bluff with only your property and even though!

Commit into hard work even where!
Earnings aren't enough, be content!
For torture chambers in prisons await
The gates are flung open so evade theft
These gates are beckoning greedy gangs and gangsters
Dominated by jealousy and greed
On the other hand
Could it be the product of society?

Is it due to promising what one cannot accomplish?
Or other factors that you cannot escape or condone
Is just the concept that you must do or have?
Do what you get from that theft solve your problems?
No need but they only escalate and in streets
You may die a disgraceful death by torture.

3 June 1993-23 July 2007

TERRORISM!

Is the era of terror ending or accelerating?
As all aren't errors but deliberate acts annihilating
Terrorism is torment!
Never resting assured are the people

Terror at home and out on the road
Terror at the airport
Even in flights, news reports
Amidst crowds wailing in blood!
The resort of the terrorists is terrorism
In revenge postures
Political, social, or religious!
However, it isn't worth so much.

Planning day in, day out, these criminals!
Causing uncertainty and insecurity
Terror at sea and across rivers!
Terror within armoured cars*
For they indeed harbour terror
Notice terror everywhere and in everything!
In games, in parties, and in halls of joy

Come out in the open
Show up terrorist, terror executioner
Know you dare not expose
For as a complete coward you trance,
Always undercover
Your days are dawned!
Terrorists in terror!
Mothers of horror and grief!

7 June 1993-23 July 2007

THE VOYAGE 7

Not that of Columbus
But I kept on moving, rigid motion packed ridden
On sceptical departure, I continued moving hidden
Frequent chill of sorrow, of my would be target
My destination in gloom!
In question: my recipients reactions my mind's preoccupation
Went I, on ahead hooked
Shall they receive me in respect and at ease?

I usually felt that here again I am going
From the east to west, deviating north-east then south
The voyage in conflict, I anchored at rest in doubt
Still the agony prompted, keeps on urging
As my mind's power subsides
So weak to move!
Another mind a subsection tells me to stay or go
I fear to leave them behind
If so I would be blank.

Would I be right, in my own right to declare?
Predestination or destiny carried, would I dare?
The trend, tugs me in jigsaw I severed inside
Thus I am being led, I believe in God's trend
Again without my safety my family I missed
So do I have to go ahead or no need?
A notion of nausea

Where would I be minstrel? Tell me.
In emptiness I am, in this voyage lonely
I doubt whether my feeling is reciprocal
Within me and them my company between
Are they my friends or foes?
I doubt in this voyage and in chill of course.

June, 1993 23 July, 2007

THE FEELING

Why hiding away from them in doubt?
Their eyes I do fear and the piercing words uttered out
From mouths that mind not their business
Note that they hide and talk about your deeds
They investigate your actions and reveal.
Research on what you do
If good, they feel jealous and boo.

If bad, they hate or mock at you and hackle
Sometimes they dig deep and tell you
They also forget about themselves in regret
Warn them to mind their business
Discuss matters of importance such as ideas
Propel into development and thrive in dear.

Stop that gossip backbiters of the innocent souls
Hiding my secret in my heart, I suspect foul
Thus I hide indoors
In fluctuations I talk and adjust in jokes
Just to evaluate and entertain the few
Those who listen and then revoke!

Remarking in spite of my running and hiding they come in groups
And then I entertain sometimes I travel far
Away but still they wait
And thus await and remain feeling far
My thoughts in delay differ!

7 June 1993-23 July 2007

UPSET-PHOBIA

The tension in timid realization of actions, upset!
No company in damp grey slumps
Reptiles eroded off their scales
Insects lose their wings absurd, in odds and roam to death
Some hang and swing in spider webs trapped
Snakes sneak around unnoticed as death, venom deadly.

Frogs, snakes' preys, jumping to escape
Hiding from me but I still fear
The cold touch an omen, a taboo to discuss
It is now a rooted phenomenon, apart and insecure
In slumber and in dream, the fear drags.

Unravelling my shattered nerves
Imagine a damp grass mash, in a corner cool on your back
The taboo of darkness thickens, in wall cracks the geckoes
Oh! In phobia! Nervous breakdown, the shrill creak of crickets
Jump, in a nutshell it chills, my blood current jerks.

This is the phobia! Crawling on my skin pore hair stands!
As the unseen creatures move above iron slabs
Between or within bric-a-brac in a slumber
I do sever when I attempt to be heroic
Hating the image
In that shadow
Attempting a threat
To my nerves!

10 June 1993-23 July 2007

THE CHALLENGE

The attempt to condone in silence, silence doubled
Thinking in deep thought I sodded, my aim in target in a jumble
In few occasions I am joyous, in other times in nervous recess
The thought of remedy!
Effort clears my way, in progress.

Challenge of the power of my will.
Could this be the end?
My wishes in reject! I stand stout and extend.
Independent of foreign thoughts
In life, challenges are numerous.
Test the strength, of greatness, in valour.

Power demonstration, rejection of basic necessities, unless!
Rejecting them in hunger strikes, all to make them understand
Allow me to succeed in this challenge of will I stand!
The challenge of denial of oneself, of wants
The urge of passion in orbit!

The bitter journey continues in this misty joy
And does this have to last so long in my experience?
Come up and stand aloof in this final attempt
I am in reject; I want to be identified in my hopes in vain
Time to follow up every bit of each separate posture
For the powerful mind
Challenge is comfort and victory so sweet
Of course a bitter comfort.

10 June 1993-24 July 2007

RESTRAINT

Do I grip the reins of control, of battalions?
My actions, undertakings to command virtue
In this atomic, nuclear, and napalm threat
The devils' intelligence is vicious!

So get things under control and avoid hazard
So that you are sure to rejoice without grief
Today's massacres in the news reflect on 'Harebell' in Liberia!
Please restrain from this bath of blood.

In tears I plead, to mankind to control
Please restrain and reflect
That this world is but temporary
Where can we resort to, to promote peace?

Mercy to human beings in race conflicts!
Here I stand helpless in my hidden views
Suppressed not to pass on
To reach your eyes in tears

Blurred by frequent tear gas
To be heard by your ears
Deafened by bomb and dynamite blasts
And I know that they have been constantly suffocated.

By flashlights and sounds
The flash of the guillotines in the hands
Of the devil is indeed evil!
Restrain therefore from that devil scourge.

12 June 1993-24 July 2007

STOP BLEACHING!

It makes me feel sick
The causes a general solder
Taking the boredom, the expenses involved
It is a crime against humanity

What is the cause or the cost?
Just to remove your lovely skin cruelly
Black is beautiful, don't you know*
Don't be so doorsill madam
Feel confident in your colour
This natural colour is your complexion.

An attempt to remove it is indeed a crime!
Be warned, madam bleacher
Do you need love, acceptance, a partner?
Do you want identification?

Whoever, whatever the reason or the cause!
It is never worth to bleach
The chemicals you use smell
It stinks; your skin hurts and then rots
Don't you know it burns and then bruises?

The upper layer of your skin is vital
Maintain it in natural texture
That is what pays
Conscious men, those who love with reason
Shall never accept you
As you the bleacher
Disintegrates alive!

5 April 1994-24 July 2007

THE ISSUE!

Life goes on unchecked it seems
Double deals are rampant
Be it the winners or the losers
You are alive and have the right
To live, to question, and to survive

Today's issues! Are they for money, power, or knowledge?
Does it count?
Can they be the providers of happiness?
Never except when blended with righteousness
Could lead to a social chaos

Dealers in business use money as power, with people
Politicians' power is the polls with people
Elites' power is knowledge amidst people
Each in its place
Must be by the consent
Of the people, by the people and for the people!

Life goes on untouched
It seems still
Others' ending is the commencement of many
In bad times chaos cause catastrophes
Come my friends and work as people
Feel your lives as people
Be yourselves and have no fear of people
Fear is for one, the Creator not people
And that is no one but God!

5 April 1994-24 July 2007

THE STRAW THAT CAME LAST

An instinct immature allowed growing
The weight of the heavy load of this trend
Climax of acceptance at limits of slavery
Every soul has a maximum power
Beyond which patience is lost in a state
Of which not all the waters of oceanic waves
Could extinguish! Thus came riots!

Not that which broke the camel's back
In poems and poetic language is camouflage
To become complicated, in logical transpositions
In proverbs as they deepen in language

That's the view of elites in practice
Close those doors of cool bureaus
And match out, join the struggle or
None shall remain in the sun for another
Shares must be fair and balanced.

Relieve them carrying that load that way
Breaking innocent backs
Only a notice to notify those who could not understand
That too much of stress leads to explosion
That rise to uncontrollable standards.

12 June 1994-24 July 2007

SUNDIATA KEITAH

Depicting from past realities, I reflect
In historical mirrors, the hero of Manding
Against susus, was an episode of the past
A remarkable historical event extract
This was in kirina AD 1235

Griots praised and still praise their thrilling manding julu
That Sundiata never ran
For he came to eradicate the susu king
Kanteh Sumanguru the then susu king
Kanteh Sumanguru the wicked tyrant

Here, rulers of today could seek knowledge, reference
No and never shall dictatorship thrive
For since in history none had ever
Tragedy, is always and had ever been
The tragic end of wicked rulers

As Sundiata sped on forwards, towards
Deadly enemy Sumanguru, yelled
Roving in dust, in that rhythmic gallop
Heroes on stallions, astride to fight
Fighting to win freedom from Sumanguru
Fanta as the spy who brought the message
That determined the enemy's omen, end.

The white cock's beak fixed on to the splint of an arrow
Aimed by Sundiata
An aim that never missed
The cry of the devil echoed
His means were thus damaged

Pursued into a cave
Where, only, everlasting hero of manding emerged
Mali erupted into an empire,
So vast free of all swords of suppression.

12 June 1993-25 July 2007

FREEDOM

The meaning of which many are ignorant
So many have been burn entrapped
We need freedom for survival
Freedom to utter out our feelings
Through which we converse in truth
Whence freedom comes, it's void to fear.

So much rampant are killings of innocent souls
Entangled in chains
Padlocked and wrapped
The key of that padlock
Thrown into deep sea
In search of that key
The mission continues
Just to search for this liberty
We need liberation
From hounds howling

Black brothers worldwide crying
For freedom of their right to talk
Up to USA and South Africa
Worst of all our fellow brothers
Cause our treachery
They must halt and stop
People!
Rise up!
To seek and toil
For freedom!
No matter how risky;

12 June 1993-25 July 2007

FLUCTUATING ASPIRATIONS

No limitations, no static decisions, raking madly for solutions
We would enquire what would we do in logic
Through instinctive guide
By waves of boredom, in search of mental freedom
We rather envy them in their reality faculty free
Free in mind, body, and soul, in thought and action
Satisfied fools reside in ghettos and gossip
These dreads in dreams are eclipsed
Amidst tragedies dreams roll-on, everlasting comfort!
Alcohol baths, destroy disintegrating bodies
Sponges soaked in these pools, hope for relief that never comes.

In that dream that may be one day, right away be rich
Driving a fleet of cars at top speed in temporal glory
Along a dimly lit tarmac road drunk and dose, dive and jive
Off track, down that ditch a quick death!

Over that blue, green, red, or even white, ultimate colour kettle bobbling green herbs
Laughter, ha! Ha! May their souls rest in peace?
That greedy group still craves and gambles
Another day the diseased forgotten
Bleak hopes moving on wards towards crowds
In economic recess, rush about in haste to deal
Taff taff! Generation struggle staggers onwards
Discuss! International conferences, defusing events of the past and present
Never silent in all but never attend to any.

Those in power aspire to torture
Racial degradation in these societies of today
Ethnic cleansing in certain parts of this globe

Religions on threat, to silence advocates or preachers
Linking earth and heaven, fundamentalists swear and fight

We attempt to condone terror
Within the inertia of hope and dismay
That horizon holds no remedy
For the human race
No refuge in this struggle
Subjects fluctuate as merciless maroons
Aspire for higher alters in vice!

22 June 1993-25 July 2007

STRANDED WANDERER

Deriving in deep dig he thought
Could all this be what it means?
Life always in fear and the question
The quest of confidence and assurance
Without doubt to live free.

The wanderer got stranded in a foreign land
Within his mind as thick as dough
As they approach him, he shivers
Now and then in this consistent tension

Do loving carry meaning in this state?
Constantly in bitter ecstasy
Attempting deliberate risk, to be certain
All this risk is null, in misunderstanding
Humanity responses negatively
Then on what shall this wanderer embark?
Hope in faith and shall righteous confidence guide

The confidence to reign, without fear
And those who dwell in it, never shall rule
They become a leader or ruler in critic
Ridden into compete nervous break
This wanderer is in lust in fading deep confidence
So shall God rescue him, aloof in surprise!

30 June 1993-25 July 2007

CONFIRMATION

Achieved at birth from the Supreme Being
Why do we need to struggle for temporary recommendation?
For the bird feeds its babies
All because she could fly to and fro
No constant accounting
Nor monitoring of where they belong
When they grow up
Fly at random directions and destinations.

Some are carried away and baffled
By baseless promises of future prospects
No clear perspective!
This I assure
My peers in doubt
Strongest hope on God
For He confirms from heaven

Feel rest assured of this promise
Avoid hoping on mere humans
Their prejudice always overtakes
Achieve the highest alter of life
Always in faith
Cling to that abstract
But strong hope
Dangling!
Swinging!
To salvage the righteous
In truth!
Thus ascend to the safe
Throne of a secured life

30 June 1993-25 July 2007

REPATRIATION

The exhale of Babylon, in blaring nostrils, they met in no fun
We need them not anymore!
They cried and complained
Economic recession on the rise
Can't you see or hear?
Out to hustle for wealth, our brothers
Scanning across seas, far beyond our borders

Far away from home into racist Babylon
Running away from us to uncertain safety alone
Trapped in camps
Claiming asylum or awaiting departure in calm
More! Back home, they must, no alternative
No reason acceptable, no need to stay
Your errands are ended
You are shocked at a halt

Away from home your hopes linger in suspense
Be assured, that here no misty mood
No hiding around corners, no request of the pass, boredom
So come back in pride, in time your land beckons you
Come! Come home and rejoice not alone
For the selfish Babylonians are enraged
No more Europe side brother, on track.

Be proud of your land so sweet
Afar you are a foreigner in bondage
Be sure to stay and work
Till the land that your forefathers chopped
Stay within reality courageous heroes
Poverty in freedom but safety at hand
Here neither race nor personality counts

But today, I say to you, go!
For poverty is a crime
Even more is a fang
Worst still, poverty stings
So go and try now
Just remember to call
Finally come home even without
The wealth you once dreamt of.

11 July 1993-25 July 2007

IN THE OUTSKIRTS

Wisely scampering away at a sudden jolt
The fierce dogs barking in rage to hunt
Cunning is this creature,
In ears vertically erect!
Skip and hide in dives
In the shrubs a prey

A whirl of dust on its trail
The race in commence
Inner circle around
It is rabbits' hunt
As boys grip twigs and follow the trend and
In this pursue, they are so eager to catch
The heat of the sun burning hot
Just like embers at the smith's workshop
Out there! Burnt down fields ease the race
Where trees lose leaves
And are left to die or live.

Thrilling is this race
A pursue to catch
The creature out manoeuvres and escapes
Out in the openness hidden
Behind shrubs
Back to the start
The hunters and their dogs
The dogs in shame
Of their failure to catch
Calmly growl as their tails sandwiched between and
Within, their arced hind legs
Of course in shame lying

At their master's feet
Panting, hah! Hah! Hah!
Subdued after the failed mission

12 July 1993-25 July 2007

THE STORM! I FELT ITS EFFECT

The rambling of thunder in the horizon yonder
Denoting another assignment of floods
Targeting an already soaked land
Marked with deep galleys
Where water rushed through

Above a mash of clouds gradually gather
As they malinger high
Above in that sky eager
So eager to pour down
Their content as they shifted
Occasional flickers in brief flames or flashes
Natural lasers as signs of
A storm as a threat!

Not assured are the dwellers in huts
Mud walls cemented with cow dung
Retreating in corners
Rearranging belongings
Threatening those under-thatched roofs
Those mud-walled hamlets

Good for our yield
In future bumper harvests
But insecure for certain weak shelters
At risk of damage
Although some may rest assured untouched
Beware you sheltering safe!
Of the helpless losing their homes
As the storm gathers in stages

Meteorologists measure speed of the wind
Gauging the level of this pouring rain
However, safe shelter is our major need
Shelter security in peace of mind
Or our homes may collapse an remain in debris
As mud, surely soaks in water.

14 July 1993

DILEMMA IN JUSTICE

It is shocking to be denied one's right
Just as tennis in a bewildered court might be
Pouncing back and forth
As Ping-Pong, inspired I hoped
Reaching my destination in the mist
Then to the head of that region
In a twisted twirl of timing

Back to my starting point
As I staggered in sceptical steps
My sceptical mind changed and charged in trends
But just for a while or so
Skipped into the trend and dropped into a trench
Thus the long wait came by
As my blind leader commanded
Insisting to save my honourable carrier in tilt
Against my will

This jolt left me numb and staggering unsteadily
Steadfast my steps resisted as I tried to flee
In the pendulum track of repetition
My mind got stuck and lingered a far
Letting all eyes witness
My safety on stake
Ecstasy my rescue
In limbo it is dread.

All is yet to be, heard or seen!
For the end is near, no hope
Unexpected rectifications, enlarged further
From all that which shatters our hope at hand
Threats from the head of that empire!

I am the subject in that empire, in shock
Where hope is lost I continue to plead for mercy
My cry for safety is yet to be heard
For those ears shield with wax are deaf
To my subdued echoed call entrapped!

17 July 1993-19 October 2007

A VICTIM ON THE MOVE

What formula can solve this quest?
Requesting for hideouts in this constant quest
People on the roads
On tracks and bush paths
Just as they all grip the base to depart
Trying to escape
This threat of being smashed

By the rampant numerous invaders
Have to be on the move
Of course no doubt
Not because they fear
But instincts act as triggers
Setting off rebellions against injustice
Innocent lives on stake!
Displayed on stages or scenes

So run, my colleague! To plant your seeds
For whence they breed in future we hope
You guy on the move, I understand your motive
For the savages are mad and ready
Just to eliminate or
Kill in cold blood and hang you in joy.

Inhuman are their aims
Their thirst quenches in your blood
Only then can the savage sleep in peace
Whilst the savages meat, is your poison
So just run if you cannot hide
As far as you could
Just to escape being devoured into doom.

25 July, 1993-19 October, 2007

THE DREADING JUNGLE

Do I dare to enter and get entangled?
My nerves freeze in this risky entrance
The heart dropped down to my boots
At the natural gate mingled are plants.

Tall trees, centuries old on that tower
Those towers that bear the fruits of venom
Within, hidden are creatures in valour
Power Is in hiding, dormant in nature

The art of the supreme creator
Wonderment so rampant in sight
In this site, no coward can penetrate
Indeed, involved are many dangers

For amidst creeping plants are snakes
There, they mingle and their colour dazzles
Making the nerves of aliens shatter
Thus I grip my armoury for self-defence
To protect my own as many others do.

But not to kill without reason
For in this jungle are other intruders
Coming in to shoot
Only to quench
Their greed
So save the fauna and flora.

31 July 1993-19 October 2007

SOTOUMA'S SWEET SECRET POOL

That the hyenas dug up the pool
Water gushed out as those creatures pulled
The grip of their paws claws revealed a message
All amidst, dry land, in a sacred corner passage

In Sotouma in the Far East end of this land of Kambi
Three decades ago, the same spot spouted
Water sprung and healed even leprosy patients
This water remedied problems in miracles
Oral messages went far and wide
Up to Guinea Conakry, Mali Bamako, Senegal Dakar, all rallied.

As the crowd rushed to see and subdue
In secret they whispered their wishes to the spirits
Of the Sotouma sere pool
Please, Mr Spirit of the pool
We ask for salvation from evil.
Enlarge my luck and offer me prosperity.

All races non-classical mobs met to sacrifice
I saw all types
And kinds of status-quo on the track
The highway leading to this pool makes no fool
The surrounding was so full
Of the socially depressed
Deprived or as they mentally believed.

Their fears, their hopes, their intentions
And mine, too, exposed to the pool of Sotouma sere
All and sundry narrated to this pool
Finally Sotouma's periodical popularity faded

This was just an era to recall
But were my prayers answered?
Yes, partly!
Now I await more positive results
As in each stage of one's life
There remain more to acquire
So Sotouma pool wet or dry
Please reunite my family
Assure me a healthy and longer life.

1 August, 1993-19 October, 2007

AS IN A CLASP!

The tipsy divvy cajoles
As directions and orders
Ramble about in jolts
Up I ascend the hills
Down I descend them
Are there any more to depend?

No! None indeed in this tedious malinger
My soul in hunger
Uncompromising tender torment
There are other souls
Aboard the wreck
They say they threaten hardened souls
So come my saviour
Amidst this rubble
I await your highly needed intervention.

Although I grip this rope
It is just a tiny thread that dangles
Thus in danger
I lament at heart in bitter silence
My kids I miss amidst my family
As they wail and I cry in loneliness
In shock they sob
As hopes get dashed
By the merciless bureaucrats
What hypocrisy!

So in faith for only in that we rely
When is the time to prove?
As crooks malinger
In search in darkness to salvage
We the parents their victims
Thus in the limits of sanity

Oh! There in the horizon hidden are hopes of joy and laughter
All but one of those may arise to win one day
Just for once, infirmness I pray
As I always did
And shall keep on doing
Until Allah the most reliable
Ordains this reunion
Long awaited
Hoping it will soon be
And thus we live once more
Together and forever more

17 August 1993-25 July 2007

THE ADDRESS

Warning to those who deny the call
Who cramp on the lives of the innocent
The beings on threat helplessly struggle
Their tongues locked at a jam, buckled
For even the words they utter aren't heard.

For hunger is the vice that retards power
These come and go
Hungry and dizzy
Thus they stagger
Dissatisfaction is the order of the era
Warning! Once more to those who are deaf
Artificial deafness!
A deliberate scorn
Can never hear

Leaders in the forefront
Please turn around
Listen to the groins of the hungry mass
Following you suit
Comes what may!
In this address time will tell
Addressing those artificially blind
Not by nature
But by deliberate act

Scorn snobs, a kin to scorpion stings
The stings of snobbery attached to them
On those hopeless
Who need attention!
Although humble and silent

But so much is their eminent suffrage
All on condition that
Mercy is obtained
Without hesitation!

17 August 1993-25 July 2007

CRITIC

Intermingling he mixes with us to investigate
Capitalizing on the slightest error, just at the gate
He watches on unabated, forward to move on
Note, not to submit false information on board
Character assassinator,
In a carrier of doubt,
You are aloof.

You may be challenge but never relax to prove
Prove him false or he thrives on and bluffs
Claiming errors of others, at the entrance
Other subjects unsure as they trance
Be sure to prove innocence or you get stained.

A mark that when he stamps, gets eternally painted
Would widely transmit into ears eager to hear your faults
Thus rank and files jubilant ignorant though
As they jump to unqualified accusations
Some or the majority are saints
The few he traps never escape him dignified.

Mr Critic, are you quite sure!
Of those stories in your reports
Causing chaos and catastrophes
Are you aware of the lives at stake?
Caused by your hypocritical sermons?
Guide your tongue, Mr Critic
Rise up your pen just a bit

Put of you hidden recorder
For a mere spy you remain
In assumption you depend
I for one assume!

11 April 1994-Sunday, 05 August 2007

ASSOCIATE

Influential associate
Announce, yourself!
In your company contagious you are
Keep away from such
Habits unworthy to emulate are poison!
None have we been born with.

Within that environment it lingers
Plainly exposed
Automatic stigma of society
Others may lucky to escape
The sweeping challenge
With wills that stand firm
No easy penetration
Of those in divine protection
Caution you, in pure sanitation.

Not to be engulfed by this tornado
It's full of pests that sting with pain
Though at the beginning
The sting makes the starter dizzy
Transmission of dogmas
Ideas! Onwards it moves
It is a living wagon.

Picking up only the seeds of society
Eye mark your neighbour and be more aware
Does he carry the venom?
That's contagious
Be it a habit, a way of life or disease
Caution is indeed a need!
Before any complete commitment.

11 April 1994-Sunday, 05 August 2007

IMMINENT ALTERATION

Here I face you my enemy!
Alter or perish is the option on my path
To whom shall I bestow my chances?
My hope to obtain
My hope to achieve this goal

The hope to escape definite infinite pain
Of course destruction is sure
If I don't
If do not halt the habit
My will seems dormant
Unable to face the challenges

Fear is my hindrance!
The fear of my thoughts
Of what is going to be
To be done
That in case I quit you.

What is my substitute?
I can't see or even visualize, rationally
What is my exact next of kin?
In case I quit this hazard, you!
A hazard that sticks like glue

And mentally my mind vacates
As my wallet and hands still purchase venom
All in my mind's denial!
I wish I never knew you
Hoping to have another
Thus I gather momentum,
To quit you, at the right moment

26 April 1994-Friday, 19 October 2007

FAREWELL APARTHEID!

This has been a dream
Though now comes true
In spite all threats of those hounds
The dawn of South Africa's cock arrives
The media crows as people wail
In bullets, heading on to the poll in courage!

Have faith, my invisible brothers
For invisible you stand against your enemy
Apartheid for centuries on end
You the monotonous hag!
A monstrous octopus
Your robes now in rags
Hard to gather!
Shattered your armoury
Is scattered into tits and bits!

Now pick up your dangling chains and perish
Those that have bound your feet
Your arms your limbs
Your muscles weakened
No more room for manoeuvre
Go! Now! Go! Forever, fade away.

We need you no more,
Your role is overdue now
For even Israel rejects
Your baggage's destiny is in the pacific
Deep down in that deep ocean
Nailed in steel box
Tight on to a heavy, huge, boulder!

For your sink and disappearance is so certain
Carpenter caution to shield the box with proper lead
So that no more could the venom of apartheid leak out
To pollute future generations
Bravo! Mandela bravo!

26 April 1994-Friday, 19 October 2007

FADING ABSTRACTS

Every thought formulates in minds', scenes!
Responded in scripts worth meaning
Where left to fade useless
Worthless, even swaying
The biggest ship at anchor
Unchained shall sift away
That floating object moves
Away and out of sight

All things end, disintegrate
Thus pass away in flights
Why this greed even in abundance?
It is bait in wait
A sweet bottle of drink
Drank, now empty, leaving mere taste
Temporary in movement it is gone, wasted
Cotton trees demonstrate
That trend in buds!

Flowering red, yellowish green fruits drying pools
Heated these crack out dry
Dismantle as filets soft
Come out escape and fly away
Natural flight, in dispersal go, light relieve
Directed by the winds
Nature on course, brief!

Transported in nature's please
Drops down at choice, in grips as twigs tease
Their they lay and wait for rain
That falls and they grow up,
To tall trees in cotton
Again as they bloom, start to fade.

Grow and die, natural or by man's matchstick
Struck to light!
Crumble and die out, late!
Dry up wilt!
Deteriorate and fall in drift
No more green
So no more life for trees too

2 May 1994-Friday, 19 October 2007

UNIQUE LADY

My unique lady, I beckon you
I wish you were to stay too
Now on the verge to vacate untouched
Your heart's content I wished to voyage through.

I feel in dismay, my thoughts and aims standstill
In ecstasy I remain, in vain, my hopes dashed, nil
Thus remain incurable, aghast in my feeble heart longing

Your speech, eyes, your personality superb
Been my dream to lodge within your arms my apology
Your ambition to serve in complete mission stagnates
Unique character, you trance in confidence, adored

Had I the Vito, I would command, steadily
What can't be helped must be endured, lady
Maintain your mind's will and firm you stand
Courage, your resort, our residence, in future more hope

My view in review, though minute
Accept my sincere plea and excuse my thoughts
For in mistake I stand, yours the truth
Go or stay the latter I prefer.

Final order returns to God
So in good may our creator guide?
In best of destinies may both of us last
Whoever the lucky guy
I wish you eternal love
Hence you should always
Remember me as I shall always remember you.

10 May 1994-Friday, 19 October 2007

THE DEPARTURE

She sobbed, plea, wailed, and cried, at last
Unbelievable she is gone
And is it forever?
I hope though not, my initiated love
Are you really gone?
Gone! No love now, no indeed not
For your image, that face, remains, in my mind

My hearts man's the reason I can't cry
Lodged deep in my heart
Real woman, how up there? Lonely I am sure if not fooled
Indeed I hope even for a second, you could recall
Those brief moments, we have shared
Intimately humane they were.

I hugged you
Tenderly in that misty end
And I kissed and kissed again
In that dusty dark street!
Beneath that mango, in tears
Then I knew surely
For you are to go!
Here I remain waiting
Hoping not in vain

Ready indeed to respond to maximum
Even forever to remain yours
And you lady
Remain mine, my woman confirmed
Your last call
At that I had to detach.

Then walk away
For saying goodbye was impossible
Your name, image, and humaneness remains
Haphazard, I am, until that day
That we could touch and embrace
One another eternally, I wish god helps us
Accomplish our love pending and afar.

16 May 1994-Friday, 19 October 2007

CAMOUFLAGE!

Lipstick art expert
In a sway at that busy mob
To whom and when are your expensive targets?
Busy brains can't see your marks
Your display to be seen in vain

Relaxed in skin polished in a glitter
Readjusted braces with necklaces that dangle down
High on heels that pierce
Humble earth's rocks and soil
Paces slowed in sandy catches
Difficult motion, just to camouflage subjects

Of course in view in these scenes
No associate in mobs of piety
Within which your calibre get tarnished
Your scalps roofed in dead, bushy
Black or reddish furry!
Goosed hipped
Tight at waist as your struggle continues

Along, fingers loaded in varied wrings of colour
Are they bronze; copper, brown-coloured even zinc
Your domestication in excess foul
Listen to this call
Could you even purify anymore?
As you drawn into extra luxury fakery
Down to earth camouflage!
Known is your colour
Your true colour is exposed now.

18 May 1994-19 October 2007

TERROR FROM SPACE

Is this a UFO in quest of their vision?
Rushing without any delay, in forward motion
Beaming, bright, gliding in blinding glow down
Towards Mother Earth, awaiting alone in frown
Here then comes mans toughest challenger
Image! An imaginary image of terror hovering
In search of landing, it is danger.

Down it came in wings, at a rush!
As a bullet but more of rocket trust
Like a meteorite, striking forward
Down to mankind's helpless rotating floor, oval, spherical
Unwanted visitor, go away, strange and horrifying
Never in human history have eyes seen such
This occurrence, in challenge
More risky than the nuclear bomb

This blazing disc, glittering in naked flames of annihilation
Wild fire, down in it came inspired commotion
Precise landing indeed it did but far for some
Thus on to, near some engulfed covered in one mighty fall
Bar rump! On no-man's-land bewildered
Man in courage challenges this terror in confrontation
Of course, no match for man, incompetent they stood at end.

The end! As the beast smiles shocking grim lighting
Across nations, continents, shaking oceans in to waves
But to no avail

What's next then, doom seem to arrive
Partial are the scenes of total fear
The end of all fear even for the hearts of cowards
The cords of their feeble hearts cowed
Twitching on and off and the courageous thrive on.

5 June 1994-Friday, 19 October 2007

IN RAGS THEY SHOW OFF

It makes the seer wonder about
What makes them dress so in ridicule?
In time past, grow-with-am and balloon shirts, flew
These were at least better
For they exposed smaller
Now a day in tights they flower.

Looks awkward in young ones, on display of muscles
These aren't forever
Remember as you bloom in your hay days
Thus trance in half-naked dresses
Up to navels?
Or up to knees?
Some they call snicker-bookers accompanying bare breast.

And are they on discard of minds or of passions in doubt?
Or just for their nakedness in display
Is this worth a bluff?
Oh boys, my girls!
Warning, to extroverts of parts that should be hidden
It makes me feel solder
Raga! Or are some muffins!

Hippies or are they crime lovers
Earrings dangling as we knew for females
But now for males
Bangles worn indeed in complete style roughly

Doubt ranges whether the mentioned males are feminine now
Culture please! Our culture covet demands robes
Not tourist resemblance when they do so
If and only if in search of sunlight
Beware that these, when back home transform
Ladies and gentlemen!

DUPLICATE REMOVED

5 June 1994-Friday, 19 October 2007

AUTHORITY

Pay heed to my plea, you the master of orders!
I indeed endure to reserve my idea, may be a method to render
But you knocked back a kick at your refusal
Gagged in silence aback, I must return, although thoughts remain vital
To expel and then go proper, in my confidence at your confirmation
My thoughts are raw, untouched, ventured, so caution in your motion
Virgin, they remain in jam I brood, contemplation and doubt in devotion

I looked up, unanswered, in strive to be understood
To thrive I need to narrate my claim soon
Into that deaf ear of yours I received though
Thus, in shame, I returned to my duty incomplete so
My approach in question
My efforts tarnished
My ideas doomed
Thus I still go up and on in courage but numb

Sensitivity my weakness
Then helpless in heart I respond less
Thus, where then my fault lies?
Is it in my personality and humour or in my behaviour and habit?
In the ripeness of time no question, on doubts

So instinctive mood be consoled, though dissatisfied
Self-control a tool to achieve success
As I obeyed but never allowed a complain
So have mercy on me!

A reaction, my option-thermostatic!
Someday, when that time's also set!
The alarm that calls conditions beyond control
Supreme, your ideas are they really the last say!
I doubt, for time shall be the fittest judge

19 June 1994-Friday, 19 October 2007

ANCESTORS' GRAVES SHAKEN

A plain reminder for the blind and deaf mob, a metaphor in stake
Who aren't dumb for they could talk?
Forgoing ancient wisdom handed down
Antique, old fashion, their ideas today as seen in major
Here and now, I stand out bold in support
Indeed so in no doubt, proved in your authenticity.

To prove your talents left dormant, several in the verge of eradication
Your devices, your tales over the embers of that fire you lit
Now in ashes, ancestral king, your wise rules and laws which regulated savages
Your architect in pyramids, granddad and mom
Your culture, your norms and values, guided moral
Your religion, your cults, and the deities you believed in

All in challenge today, in denial still note
That no proper substitute to all those you left for us
Your sons suffer, as you wriggle, shaking in your grave
Today's torments, suffrage, reminds
As paying the price of deviation from your golden old route
From the channels you dug for canals

All your wars of resistance we read, anti-colonial battles
Flown into the misty horizons' futile end, we today see far off
Slacken your course granny on to your off springs!
Your further pressure may lead to our annihilation
Backed by God, you are invulnerable, for no more do you fear to die
For already you had and shall no more die, as stands our dreading fear

The end of all struggles in life
The big end we all fear is death!
Your threat on us
Thus I plead and apologise for the errors
Of our generation in lust
On behalf of the ignorant, no feeling subjects of our time.

19 June 1994-Friday, 19 October 2007

SCAPE GOAT!

Who is the real culprit?
Your chances on threat
No room to explain and prove
Your impeccable innocence
Stick to your ideology no sway
Your words must stand bounds

Fortified you shall last not in the planned lust
Accused of not your crime
For no witness to back you and this they know
And undercover they rejoice
Being the real culprits they plan smartly
Culprits, inculcators, nets thrown!

Caste to catch noble quiet human
Tracing unaware of baits
Even in journeys beware of dealers in disguise
For in suspicion, they could pass
And stain your luggage with drugs in kind
For these illegal objects they live for and on.

Indeed, never wishing to associate with here we in freedom should notice
And take greater care of the nets on cast, hidden beneath
Before you get caught in surprise
When in reality you are clean
Ere, prove you may suffer without
Compensations fairly enough

19 June 1994-Friday, 19 October 2007

TURNING POINT

The rapture denoted earlier calls
Reference to 'brink' smashes humanity
The longest day has alas elapsed!

Brothers and venture on the throne
At your mercy the masses depend
Expectations accomplished, though we commence.

Comrades, we all remain to change
High indeed to all heights is the time for change
In valour, virtue pioneers boldly tarnished cold tyranny.

A system that almost looked everlasting
A dream comes true for the virtuous moment
A grief moment for crooks and cheats, indeed in fear!

Salvation dawns my people
Remain in minds tranquil
Staggering, 'kambi', now your pillars are firm.

Order of this day is the truth
So beneath your prepared shelter we resort
Patriots, on your steady chariot we board.

22 July 1994-Friday, 19 October 2007

HAMLETS DECEIVED

In dazzle I entered into the unknown
Had been a venture
Curiosity quench of lust
A surprising awareness on the scene
Hamlets really thrive in cities!

Not much far-off but remote
In comparison within this circumference
I never even dreamt
That this land of expectations do comet
Such in its midst, so lonely

I passed a right in sober tranquillity
In venture, in search of reality
Of what, does exist around
I did indeed think that such, only in the east
The oriental of my state, our country

The value I bestowed
Deceived my hopes, learnt the lesson of shock in series
When numerous, bread pleasure
Inexplicable experience
Till you trance my way.

Just off the coast
Towards which all rush
Seeking refreshment, natures fruits, likewise
Anchors deepened by most
For at arrival they naturalize.

2 July 1994-Friday, 19 October 2007

ISLAND OF MISERY

A comparison to Robin Island
My analyses may suit or fail
As I still have to clarify and leave
The spots of misery marked
Follow the trends that guide my vision.

Night rovers on trance, alert!
That you won't be misjudging
Beggars note where to seek alms
Those, who offer, feel restraint
For in quest to doubts are appropriate
To avoid duplication

Do not hesitate, donors!
Redeem those in misery
They need your health in all and sundry
Make them feel secure
Attempting not to offer with condition

Consider those in limbo
For down the ladder they remain
Do not just state and leave
Apply effort to rescue lives
For in time actions are valued more.

2 July 1994-Friday, 19 October 2007

FEELING TO EXIT

Initiating a departure
The malinger to set-off
Unsure to move
Thus I perambulate.

Converged and feverish
Within the melody of silent voices
Do they dictate a mix-up?
But just to get going, becomes an option.

Change the situation!
Try to see something new at least
Different people, their cultures, their postures, and activities
The need to change, in reluctance to stay!

However, I doubt how indeed, becomes a need
To see intuitiveness in my ego
Satisfaction of indefinite aims!
A human horizon, as a mirage, on the rise!

To me are not empty
But full of experience
For every minute that elapses matters
Ere departure, hesitation!
Destination unidentified!

28 July 1994-Friday, 19 October 2007

INVISIBLE REMINDER

From a distance, your rumbling
A uniform grumble, narrating flashes
A reminder of the beginning of all
Real nature is invisible, in this form a sample in your echo
Thunder! A hash roar rattle, gradually subdue far fading!
Such as the rolling of empty zinc can
Or an empty barrel on cement floor!

Causing things in need of your product quench in shower
Since indeed, henceforth!
Without you no real life
Counting not on appearance to be popular
The rolling sound in which
You prove your capability.

Direct link with the tiller of earth
Without your aid he tills not easily, rocky soil
Pilots deviate or unavoidably venture
No alternative in your risky path
Man in his canoe cocks ears, in deep sea

A retreat he and many more not, as cowards
In their plans to carry on
Suspense on journeys
All to evade possible danger
Unpredictable, you remain superb finally!

28 July 1994-Friday, 19 October 2007

A FAILED PROMISE

A social omen in existence
Leaving man all time suspicious
Promised, one hopes till
Out! Turns negative a hope
A shock, a light jolt

Acceptance depends on situation
As faith becomes the only alternative
For the compensation never reached
Come not my way
For no mercy
There by, no excuse.

All my deals are on sacrifice!
In trance to catch up
Costs me my love!
The comfort of home evaded
After all in vain
Back to commence.

Agreements tarnished in disappointment
Was I to gain the upper hand
The hardened heart to force or sanction
I would have applied to make sure
Not only are they failed or fulfilled
But devils paid their dues.

28 July 1994-Friday, 19 October, 2007

ON THE RUN

In echo the sermons signal, calls!
Of culprits and crooks
On the move in hooks
Uprooting roots of vice!
Just to establish brutes in line.

Hiding in moods of silence
Hidden in hoods of vengeance!
Deceiving fools with tools
Drenched in pools

Souls in cool tempo
Consoling look so
A sabotage of wolves
Matching on in hooves
For aren't wolves but horses.

Trampling on cooling grooves
On pebbles that pierce, punch, and prove
On their feet bare
The rough road races clear
Towards a no-man's domain
So keep on in trance to remain
For no matter what
Live you must.

30 October 1994-Friday, 19 October 2007

THE UNLAWFUL TRIAL

On venture I attempted
But in regret, I got tempted
To judge as human ego's tug
The pull to accomplish this tough

My emotions in array
The search of the suitable way
Means missing to commence
Do I need to declare?
Are they right to call me names?
Is it wrong to find?
Is it right to fetch?
All are right to go on a venture!

Still, in dilemma, as I miss
This embrace of value
The denial of a kiss
Then I try to express my need
Just in order to feed
This, my lonely heart!
Still, no definite target in vision

Nature calls for it
Thus I answered to it
Inevitable must
A substitute of love trust
Forward in scepticism
Of what they might say
Are eyebrows raised?
Only for this common request!

30 OCTOBER 1994-Friday, 19 October 2007

THE BIAS HEART

Preference in human nature
Just try the neutral in future
Are features stable for fortunes?
Matters on table forecast!

Within it decisiveness triggers
Judged by action or in uttered words
Or even in thoughts
Though hard to deduce them, abstract

Amongst people the one you choose
Amongst friends, you're intimate
Amongst opposite sex,
The one you get used to
Love is, however, made!
Thus nurtured forward to be mutual

Always our ego masters the course
Our wishes tarnished into thin air!
As they varnish unfulfilled
Thus in positive chances
Your favours thrive
Fixed we remain settled
If our needs are met

In pure humanity
Lodges the complain
Do not be bias
Easier said than done
For nothing but the human fault
Our passions first
So must deny their urge.

30 October 1994-Friday, 19 October 2007

THE SPIDER'S METHOD

Every human goes in semblance
The spiders method surpassing
For jigsaw
Manoeuvres at bay
In try chance
The unsure go in webs of thread.

Have tried of course
Assistance, for links
None in resemblance paid
As impatience, never allowed
For whence to try lonely
In tension to attempt
At a rush to narrate
Views as most fail.

Then expect a result in few
Mostly a shock in their response
The mad spider method
Can't just prove
Our aims of success
For the main objective remains to belong

The feeling of suspense
None belonging to get challenged
So in dismayed and disgruntled secrecy
Trying further
Just to fit
To hope and catch up
On went on
As even now going on

So many directions
Those remain unaccomplished
The deepest and most acceptable
May reject the rest
Unless those, that prove better
Chances of another link
These may be too good
For targets' consciences

30 October 1994-Friday, 19 October 2007

DO WE NEED IT?

Your way of life is yours
What you feel about us matters not
I heard of you since
Had read about you in history
The subject I didn't bother to master
For it made me sadder
From Julius to Napoleon
I scanned through those bitter pages
Narrating how you came, saw, and conquered
Just mustered to have the surface view

As even those records you kept
Were in doubt for the facts of history
Thus I embark on this search
To find out whom actually I was
How much I could do, think, and plan
Thus develop my own way
In my pure thoughts

What is wrong in being I?
To know for now I know
An African, a black!
Aren't I human too?
So in grip I hold my spade to dig out
The depth of my land, boldly
Every hour, every minute, and every second!

The whole of my breath to prove
My pure innocence, my ability to build
Untapped knowledge
Independence I need
That which you tamper not with
In domination of my sovereignty's worth
So slacken your sanctions now

30 October 1994-Friday, 19 October 2007

DOMINATED MINDS

As foreign dogmas were stocked
In the archives of colonial masters
Doctrines thrived in their schools of thought
Though these got implanted in our old minds

These helped the smart or lucky to escape
And a total captivity that doomed the unfortunate
The majority became seeds of exploitation
As symbols of patriotism got tarnished!
They were taught to divide and rule
In disguise to satisfy colonial rulers and their pioneers

Who became answerable to the foreign call!
Those even now receive slaps of shame
Vacate my land!
You the minds, of dictation!
Allow those free of the colonial imperialist
To hold the reins
To rule our land

Out-dated personalities in discard
Come not my way
For that boils my blood
In my already charred veins
Leave our ambitious minds
Those real minds
To watch and understand

To undertake the task of liberation
And enjoy the fruits of freedom
It is still not too late to depart
For that could benefit our future leaders
For those of today are on threat

30 October 1994-Friday, 19 October 2007

NO MATTER HOW

Much do we ponder!
Do we plan for wonder?
Still we trance to catch up
In this rat race
Obtain what's in need on top
Or keep on trace.

So do we bother to consider!
That which we seek for
Is furthered, yonder!
It may be at hand
We are just waiting for a chance
Thus searchers!
No need to chant.

Stick not to complicacy
Jams thoughts even in frivolity
Notice that to achieve we must
Our goals but a must
To believe and trust

This we label, chance
For only God can enhance
Our needs to revive
Not only to survive!

26 April 1995-Friday, 19 October 2007

AT THE HEM!

The brink of things denote, ends
Recommencing circuits in circles, bend!
As life, alive, slides in curves!
Like flying multi-coloured doves on flight

Notice that those trends are fenced
Terminated at borderlines in defence
To turn and run away isn't heroic adventurer
Struggle and undo to discover

All things are hemmed
That's no tempt
Proven in fields universal
Endless U-turns though apart

May mean territorial
Judgement's hems in trials
An entire world shakes up
For the hems are always on top
Or at peripheries
Completely surrounding
Humanity in series
Of endless stories!

27 April 1995-Friday, 19 October 2007

THE MOVING DEAD!

Not those already in graves
The cemeteries shaken
As tombs crack open, in stakes
Is it not so, lay man?
In our officials' eyes
A probing labour

On the roads!
In street corners carrying loads
The actions and appearance of these victims
Mark some are indeed pimps!
Teamed in camouflage coverage
As most humans dwell in courage

Internally rotten though
Cosmetics disguise within
Struggling on they move undecided
Prompt death guaranteed indeed

Surprising most of those
Who never expected
Long have they lived?
Amidst us in neglect
Mind them so
It is a need
All at a rush when they even feed
Neither next day let alone tomorrow
For even in peace
They privately sorrow.

29 April 1995-Friday, 19 October 2007

WHEN THE GOING GETS TOUGH!

In the toughest of times
Only heroes raise banners in triumph
Excluding gun stingers!
For amidst joy in madness
They are mere sneakers
Thus the weak and nervous withdraw
Just when refused to draw.

Contempt and scorn, amidst malice
Brooding and moving in dark allies
In wonder land trapped
Just as they try to trap
Witch hunters, incantations
Narrating sermons of doom to nations

The tough still get going
Not at bay
Neither astray
Nor in disarray
But they pray
So masters of this world of prejudice
Are those whose wills stand strong?
Swinging freely arms flung.

Strong beings still maintain strength
Even when world power claimers threaten
Bravo to the brave

You are special
In the toughest of time's trend
Stand firmer MR STRUGGLER
And never stagger
Even in chilly fever!

30 April 1995-Friday, 19 October 2007

THE DEAF AND DUMB

I wish you could talk, my mute
Although remaining kind and minute
You are so associative, my lad
You could surely understand
In mimes and signs
You send your signals.

Demonstrating what words meant final
The terminus of your efforts
It makes me sad as you report
I've noticed your generosity

Though few could maintain piety
The patience just to stop and look
For without sight we couldn't hook!

Neither comprehends nor carries out
I feel that you couldn't utter
Only a single word out
Nature controls!
Though you always attempt
Mostly in contempt
Thus you withdraw and once more remain patient
Affront these audiences' impatience!

1 May 1995-Friday, 19 October 2007

A TRIBUTE TO BOB MARLEY

Can't make it a master piece
But won't I try,
Not only to cry,
But to please!
Thus I have to accomplish this wish
Deep indeed it is.

Lest my contribution
Is a revolution
The notion to strengthen
The banner of Robert nester Marley
Bob of long time gone
Bob Marley and his spirit
Still hangs around
Surrounding patriotic modern minds
Via reggae music!

Yes! Generations yet to come
Your words Bob shall become
My heart, mind, and soul shake
And shall ever shake in joy and sorrow
If I just listen once more and reflect
Back to your precious revelations and prophecies

Your stakes, noticing all were
But prophecies and philosophical
Now, every other day proven
Factual as events unfold
Justify your philosophies
Mr Bob Marley!

Mainly focussed
On raising bowed heads
Unravelling generations
Old historical dominations
Freeing the downtrodden
Exploited innocent souls
Oh Bob Marley!
Shook up and shall continue shaking forever more
The strongest of devils
No more disguised colonialists.

Although you are gone
Your songs still haunt them
And shall drive them out of our sight
And away from our lives
To obtain the total freedom
We all deserve
Thank Mr Bob Marley
May thy soul RIP.

7 May 1995-19 October 2007

WORLD HOLOCAUSTS

Since 3945 within this century
Centum elapsed as scenes unfolded
In the path of history
Can't we see the continuing peripheral atrocities?
Worst in renowned cities
Not only did the victorious
As well the victims in the Far East

But today's holocausts are numerous
Are they in the lower degrees?
In Rwanda the Armageddon, Tutsi-Hutu, conflict
Seeming as in Yugoslavia former ethnic cleansing inflicts!
Every continent contained brutalism
As seen in cinema rituals

Now halt! Who shall we blame?
As the press makers of history claim
That the Nazis doomed Jews!
The sorrowful six million charred in chambers.

Down to Africa from cape to Cairo
The winds of holocausts in all forms persist
Sticking like the ink of biro!
Prisoners in labour camps

Refugees Armageddon in foreign threatening lands
Simmering nations!
Just waiting for commanders to fire
And now in shock!

Tearing apart sisters in rags!
As people massacre people!
Thus the constant annihilation continues
Of innocent masses
Annihilators please stop these massacres!

8 May 1995-19 October 2007

MY DARLING

My dreams roll on out-straight
The cords my heart at maximum lengths
In your heart my darling!
I surely dwell
It is eternal I swear!

Come not our path destroyer
Hypocrites vacate!
For your turn has vanished
So deep down I retire
In your bosom
As you blossom
For only God
The creator knows
How far I wish to remain yours

Prosperity and friendship!
Of course is our wish
But based on love amidst
In faith let's subdue our hopes
For heavenly you've been created

Love! Is nurtured darling
And that's exact, we trance on wishing
As those in separation wail to unite
Just for once more
Hope we shall thrive
In future, I pray
To fulfil our wish to love and live
Longer, in peace and prosperity

13 May 1995-19 October 2007

MY CATALYST

The neutralizer of my sombreness
Within your delicate soft arms
I harness
The look of your catering
Calm eyes!
Penetrating my hardened heart
Feeling me with joy
And softening my sadness
My bitterness abbey
Gone dormant
Caused by your generous attendance

Your understanding
And your reservation
These devotion and cautious attention
For you! Do not want to harass me
Always in search of my joy
I know you love me, darling.

Sure are we sure?
That this is mere earthly marriage?
No I fully deny
For to me, we remain intimate
Much more even deeper in love

After a hard day's struggle
I rush up to you my best nest!
Forgetting all threats and challenges
Until another day rises the sun
Once again for me to go and struggle
As a full man, assured by the power

And assistance of God
To come to you again and again
I constantly keep wishing
Until I heave in relief
Detached from your caressing soft embrace!
Once more back to the real world
Boldly refreshed!
To stand stronger and firmer
As our love fuels me up!

13 May 1995-Friday, 19 October 2007

TUMBLING VESSEL

When shall you go ashore?
May take longer, I am sure
Twisting and turning
In respect to the existing current
The maritime current!
As the rippling and splashing
Of tiny and strong waves smash
Your sides, proceeding in perspective
Merging the horizon
In blue, white colours.

The hasher waves do come by too
And get your sails torn to slices
The paddles slipped off rower's hands
Oh, my rocking, tumbling little boat!
There is no anchor sling
So how can we go ashore?
Could your stoppage be assured now?

No tree around
No pole to catch on to
Then you keep on turning
In rocky circles around
That rough sea
The depth of which is unknown
This breeze, not anymore cool and calm

And the land is still far away
No sign of the slightest of land
Only diving birds
Gliding up in the sky
Accompanied with dark clouds
Of a preparing storm
With sun setting at a faster rate!

15 May 1995-19 October 2007

WHIRLING VULTURES

So busy in search, in swerves
The scent of victims' gashes in war fronts
Hope my instincts and
Imaginations are right?
So high up in the sky viewing
Now numerous corpses about!

So they vultures become instinctive
Thus shamelessly selective
But do they reason?
No, not so
Incomplete innocence unaware
Evolution directs and dictates them
To maintain their flesh eating

Little children, women, old, and young
All on the Armageddon's run
Just before they collapse and die
Vultures thus come down gliding
Swiftly spiralling to survey before
They land around their dead
Prey of horror!

Mouths full of saliva
As the hungry vultures are due to flavour
Ghastly in war-torn lands
Vast vulture colonies in party
Scampering in jubilation
Whence they start to tear

The eldest start to retreat in skips
Aback just to say
'We are not so familiar to such'!
As inexperience younger ones continue
Their vicious party!
Chapping, tearing, pulling out
And chuckling human flesh
What a sorrowful scene!
An absolute evil
Caused by the dividends of war!

15 May 1995-19 October 2007

EQUILIBRIUM SOCIAL

Tipping the balance
All to enhance
Our etiquette towards others
Creating minds that match in order
Accept our natural boundaries
And our basic differences

The mastery of society
The aim to live smooth in society
Even in piety, knowledge always counts
Of course in all endeavours
Pre-knowledge guides hunters
Not ignorant military juntas.

Thus knocking edges at ends
If proposals bend
Manifestos lay in perspective
Principles and laws to execute
So must be just for all every citizen.

All just to liberate
Minds and souls that vibrate in doubt
We need thus to learn
By drinking deeper into the pools
Of knowledge and wisdom
Indeed to know
Not only how to survive
But as well to be fairly
Fit and free.

18 May 1995-19 October 2007

ONE BLOOD

Be it based on geneses
As the pious always claim and rely on
The undeniable Adam and then Eve
Be you Asian or European creed
American or Australian origin
Africa mother of races and colours!

All humanity remains semblance
Blood texture universally red
So what is the row and race about?
Of colour, in apartheid-minded beings!
Of class in small-minded humans!

From microscopic germ to maturity
None could claim freedom
Black or white
Confirm that we remain erect

Not some crawling, like insects!
Or others flying like birds
No race is superior
From the same source
All races sprang!
For sure, the end of all
Shall be death
By hook or by crook
We all must vanish in the end
Out of life
Finished!

18 May 1995-19 October 2007

AFRICA COULD UNITE BUT!

Amidst derangement and the rubble of wars
And the aftermaths of battles
We still desire and so double
Our efforts and ideas are still at large
Amidst scorn we need bold courage
Africa, multiracial, land of all
Of course, in chaotic jeopardy

Please reflect on your kindred
Wailing, suffocating in tears of blood
In battle fronts!
Escalating ethnic and tribal wars!
Toppling eras in misguided aims
Where several return to the style
Of the dictators they toppled!

The rest in the west thus return
Rushing to do business with the new regimes
To invest and mostly exploit!
By assessing our exact needs
Especially on demand of luxury
And mostly heavy armoury
For the new military dictators!
Partial tranquillities imported
Goods in mass products
Disguised as privatisation
Potential consumers, of course, import meagrely.

Aids still keep on flowing down to us
As famine stays put!
War-ridden zones
Showered in armouries!
Guns, tanks, jet fighters, rocket propellers!
All enhancing bloodshed instead of unity!
But still we prefer peace
And everlasting love with harmony

Inevitable, one day must we
All unite
For we trust
That the innocent blood sacrificed
Will never go in vain
And that the era of the just
Shall soon come to rule
To unite us all as one family
In freedom and justice for all

17 July 1995-19 October 2007

KEEP THINKING

Thought tortures raging nerves
Or instead keep them calm
Transformed into dreams in sleep
Uneasy comfort entangled at foreheads
All about outlets within the tedious

Receding or diving deep into states
Of shock, offering, submitting, oneself
Demanding, repenting errors of life
The final resort always—phoenix!

At all moments towards the supreme power
For all scenes of life are but apparitions
That come and departs
Living thinkers thinking
Brooding through life
Until they end in silent graves.

Beware, that some thoughts
Must be reserved
Piercing and echoing laughter
Dug from the depth of tired hearts
Bouncing about like irritated atoms

Reacting and living thus,
Think we must
The power source of calculated actions
Premeditated results show
And when alone the act and art
Of thinking redoubles

The average common subjects
Claim, talking to others helps
But just as you sit up to speak
The vicious, snare, and swear
To dim you down!
Drop you down,
Casting crooked sights
So no more vigour to chat
Drained so back to yourself, cooled
Thoughts, when censured
All destinies remain at a risky stake!

16 January 1999-19 October 2007

THE BATTLE OF LIFE

Being on the wrong path
At odds with time!
Living a numb life
All options applied but no outlet found
Seen amidst contradictory principles tried
These extremes keep us pulling us apart!

But the journey thrives in survival
So hard to know, what to regard
In the midst of the tug of war
As these iron ropes pull constantly
Causing strong minds miss goals

In territorial occupations
Always the odd ones out as at now
Ultimate wish to be accompanied
By the one and only
Without whom or with
Walk, search, pray, and wish I knew what!

But nerves shake in life submerged
Indeed doing what I wished
Not to do
Or must do to survive
Hating more the puff! Sip and chew
Indeed crave for what already had been attained!
Crudely though as I move through
The roughest and toughest roads

In mere cheap and
Crazy world of wars
Of less words, chorused by sounds
Of big guns' and bombs!

22 August 1997-19 October 2007

HATRED RETARDS US

The hatred driving hater's heats
It burns him out like a rat caged and lit up
You see how fire burns out a candle!
Or how fire eats up dry vegetation!
Or how it burns out dry grass even faster

The piercing tensions keep on
Circulating, thus generating a special tempo
Of fear and nervousness
Mixed up! Then boils up!

This feeling when suppressed
Ferments into gastric heat
Of malice and anger, caged

As the ringing bells of Satan sound
These sermon cords of reaction
Melting into disturbed envy
So no peace for haters!

Resting in the nest of hatred
Are the vicious demons
So hate not your fellow man
Exchange hated for love.

Eat and rejoice in peace
Feel love and no need to hate
Without hatred and malice
Love rules!
With love there is always peace
Breeds wisdom, health and wealth

5 October 1998-19 October 2007

FILLING THE GAP

This gap gapes at me fiercely
In every move, thought, and action
All just meant to subsidize the gap
A dread to stay awoken
In horror and sorrow

Thus I chew, puff, and drink china tea
Speak out or read books and papers
Listen to the radio
Have a walk and think
Stop by the shop and around my
Neighbourhood

Trying to fill this gaping gap
I mostly pray
But still remain a prey of time
For to pass it costs me
Energy and money
Thus the gap remains hallow.

Even in bed
I puff
Ere the smooth call of sleep
Comes and creeps over
My raging nerves
The only time I attain freedom
Till once again I get awoken
To this dreading gap
That openly and mercilessly demands
An already saturated satisfaction

23 August 1997-19 October 2007

TIMID DAYS!

Because of this rigid timidity
Caution in every action limited
As I a marauder still hoping
Searching for another corner
Just to do away!
I could no more visualize
As I think, talk, and walk
Shocked and totally disoriented
Side-lined, only pleased with a cigar
That even now makes me crave more.

My best, I apply in another stake
Calling on telephones!
Travelling on trains, metros, and buses
At times walking with aching feet

In sleep almost dead, no dreams
For not only the dreams
But also my limbs and my mind
Over worked in a state of employment
My only employee is the search
For a job to do

Now a drift trying to orient
With a fatigued mentality
But hope still lingers around my mind
That to make it
Would I indeed!

20 November 1999-19 October 2007

CIRCUMSTANCES

Controlling actions
Not predestination
Believe so in destiny
Kinetics in people and time

Balls rolling random on table tops
Humans act so
One ball knocking another
Which then, moves, by coincidence?

Thus move and ardour what comes
Is a world of inartistic moves?
Where chances depend on circumstances
Circumnavigating aims and about anywhere.

Where against our wills?
Resort then to pending conditions
Dictated by circumstantial moments
May the divinely power of God
Be the cause of our moves to the everlasting good.

Thus favouring them in order
Achieving the heaven on earth
And not only here but the here after
For all wish to be in heaven
By all circumstantial means!

23 August 1997-Friday, 19 October 2007

TIGHTENING UP

The more the noughts tighten,
The darker the objectives
Visiting, asking for prayers
And after every prayer
The stirring gets much harder.

Fear rules my shaky life
Short rushing contacts
Just to secure another pack!
Drinking tea more than the kettle can boil
Totally out!
Of what use to be myself
So now and then
Think of God!
Hoping for Him to rescue me

But tightening up
Knowing not who to blame
Who is blame worthy?
Really need to change
Many have talked
But nothing rather occurs
So now what next comes?
I do not really know
But for sure Allah knows
And will surely guide.

22 November 1999-Friday, 19 October 2007

WHETHER YOU LIKE IT OR NOT

Take what you have
Is the acceptance of reality?
This is always a condition
For feeling upset causes more harm
Mr Radical, please call on other's views

No matter how much or what
Expression, reaction, or deviation
What to be got to be
So why worry?

The conscience haunts the mind
For the reservoirs of deeds
Can never fade away
For stocked they are
To the culprits brain

Thus trance on honest and pray
Ultimate recipient of virtue and vice!
Only Allah, could cater for all
So ask for His forgiveness
Blessing, to lessen the heavy load of sins
Vices committed
Since they of birth
Trust the almighty could forgive
You! In doubt of Him
He is the greatest.

26 August 1997-Friday, 19 October 2007

QUITE THE OPPOSITE

Every other day, hours go by
Every other one goes along
Why not I too?

Praying all night
And sleeping the day out!
This is how nature rules me now
Going back sometimes I think!
To where and how!

This question again
And again
At mornings!
Where every passing
Minute counts.

Now my pen vouches
This authentic reality!
As knowledge hurts
When not utilized.

Awaiting for the day
Of the final explosion
Positive let it be
Come by!

Feeling like a rotten rag
With a rat wrapped inside
Wedged amongst clean clothes
In a closed suitcase

25 November 1999-19 October 2007

THE TOMORROW THAT NEVER COMES

As habits get entwined
Become part of us
Hardly changed
Seeing the vision of reason
In gloom!
Shall that tomorrow come?

Look around the corner of your eye
At the bottom of your heart
Not too far off
Is with and within!
Much of practice
Makes perfect
It's a fact.

Revising backwards may threaten
Assured progress and stability
Based on reality
Not radicalism
The time is now!
Not tomorrow
Not to be in pending state
Pessimistically receding
As never was there.

Common to realize and reason
That the consumer of time
Is nothing but procrastinations?
Burning the value of life; out
The only that
Goes by and sadly no change
There can surely be
A decisive change
If God wishes and wills!

24 December 1997-19 October 2007

WHY CAN'T YOU SEE ME?

Here again the inspiration comes!
Could you hear the cry from my heart?
The tears that drip down unseen
Can't you see my zest?
That peace on my face!
My objective for all

Can't you feel my gaze?
Every little move that I take
Towards you and everyone else
But no! None seem to understand
As in turmoil, every my action
My each move an omen
Even when I try to explain the worst!

No right seems to be on my side
Reserved within the wishes I harbour
To start correcting,
Starting with none but myself

For all I do means trying to stabilize
Get understood by whom now?
For without speech, how could I?
But when winning comes that day
Shall be the brightest and happiest day

25 November 1999-19 October 2007

BEWARE OF WHAT YOU WANT
AND TAKE WHAT YOU HAVE

Not what you want alone counts!
What you had done
Seen or felt
What you do, eat, put on, or read!
Reflect on, how you look
So what you have and are really counts

Reality is, who you actually are!
Where you believe to belong
Not only has the knowledge had you acquired
But implementation is what counts
What you do, how you act?
Do you help others?

Wants should never overshadow haves
Or denying the fact of real situations
Enhances deviation from yourself
Do not be illusive!
That illusions breed null.

Voids the contents of the skull you wear
Roofed by the hair
Couldn't be avoided
Although some attempt so
Improve on what Allah provides.

Content with haves,
Caution with wants!
Wants cause havoc not only to you
But to those you deal with too
Shift away from greed and choose
Prayers to Allah, when in need
Within the circuit of your spiritual ability
Create stability,
God's support is always assured.

20 December 1997-Friday, 19 October 2007

LOVE ON SALE

Once I was told that it's for sale
To marry one has to pay a dowry
All along I believed to win a heart
But never had such come my way

So far to attain value dollars first!
The cash most crave for, if not all
Foremost question remains
How much do you earn?

Are you employed?
What grade?
Thus to live one must have it
Make it!
Gather bunches of it, yes
Checks must be cashed!

Every thing in today's life
Therefore, money talks!
Yes, even when they say
No! People are better than money!
Hello! That I deny
For it is only hypocrisy
Now I accept the means
To many ends
Is these coins
The papers, bills, and pay checks
Yes, no money!
No way to joy!

25 November 1999-Friday, 19 October 2007

MAKE OR BRAKE

This makes me brood
To move on or stop
To be mute or speak
To be generous or stay a miser
To sit down or remain standing
Enter or stay out of view
No company, insight
To be lonely and think it out all alone

To sleep or stay awake!
Explain or reserve my thoughts
To look or shut my eyes
Hear the call or remain deaf!
Laugh or cry!

Keep on loving or hate?
Except God the almighty
But that's contrary
To His revelations
Run! To where?
Walk for time won't stop ticking
Keep a cool pace or tempo
No rushing please.

Then ease up to visit neighbours
Salute relatives and friends
Or stay put at home alone
These are the options
Remain so!
Or trigger dormancy in life
The will of this strong heart in demise

Bearing the pains
Shocks and dismay!
For horror and sorrow
Rule such beings!

22 August-Sunday, 26 August 2007

DISCOMFORT!

For every discomfort felt
Misfortune, heart-breaking
All that makes man feel
Being in the wrong place
At the wrong time, in claws
Amidst the unprecedented

Dealing with the usual challenge
Changes and interactions
In social life and business
All oppressions, orders, directives, inter
The rule of dictators, autocrats, traitors!

Under all above and others discomfort
Those in captivity, locked and behind bars
Failing marriages and soured relations
Poverty, hunger, degradation
Torturing thoughts!

And those far from their lovers' comfort
Warm bosoms, nowhere to be
Loneliness for those
Away from former good times

In discomfort too
So comfortable are the faithful
Fighting the battles of injustice
Even though in battles most
Rebels die degradingly
Warning! No easy way to success
Not a dream but reality

With discomfort we live until dreams come true
And hopes realized
Even though tits and bits remain
As memories are hardly erased
Till the grave!

Sunday, 26 August 2007

SO HELP ME GOD

Special prayers that can solve all problems just try it and see how soon things would change better forever in all domains tested and proven surely

I plead oh God
Of the universe
Come to my aid
And those of my kind
Regard not our numerous faults
Our sins for never shall
They thrive sinless, unless you guide

In ghettos we commence the search
Filling up craving gaps
Those thirsty gaps
Gaping and groping for virtue
Pure goodness we wish.

Longing to water dry deserts
As deserted hearts twitch and ache
Where rain is indeed far off
And tears couldn't suffice
To ease the tight tension

But oases are even in the Kalahari
And the Saharan sea of sand
Doon in the Namibia desert and Amazon
All couldn't compare scorching hearts

That lacks your omnipotence
So guide them and I to heaven
So help me, God
For only You
I trust!

16 September 1997-Sunday, 26 August 2007

THE DARKEST DAYS GET DARKER

Amadou bh Sey

A total silence persists on my path
Within and indeed in the midst of the loudest noise
My nerves shake every moment
The more I try to tranquilise my thoughts,
The more the storm rages
Trembling hearts drop down to feet
What a dark night!

The quest of papers rampant in chats
No reliable associate around
Only those who intimidate
Count not on what they vouch neither
What a dark night!

For under all trusted swears
Beneath a total fakery
About and bound tight
What a dark night!

Resorting home out of question
Home is indeed quiet far away
And staying equals hot like an oven
What a dark night!
Not even one!
To warm my freezing heart!
Craving for an embrace
In this first cold winter in France

Someone enough to brighten my heart
My path and the destiny of my kind in bondage
Away from home in search for better pastures
What a dark night!

Amadou Bh Sey

17 December 1998-19 October 2007

CLIMAX

I pulled all cords
But the strings remain tight
So strong and maximised
But hardly do they comprehend my plight

This plight I always plea to God
For in Him I believe the only!
Who could comprehend this complexity?
For all in jeopardy
Wretched in shape!

Move I on to people
Cool and gentle at heart
In inner peace I pray
In steady free mind of peace with God
Want I, sometimes want to explain
Just to the rare few who listen

To those I think could understand
If I think and see
As if dead men exhumed
From disturbing graves for their deeds
Deeds of vice whence they lived

I reject to be belonging
To none but God
For the best of friends
And attractive and most tempting

Colourful, all but mere fakes

Amadou Bh Sey

15 September 1997-19 October 2007

THE HELPLESS PRINCIPLE

Amadou Bh Sey

Wait and see in wonder
Trying to advance in venture
But most imagined obstacles hinder

Be ready on alert hustler
This is an ascending zest
Towards an anticipated success
Propelling at knots but static after all

So tough and hot towards the core
A twisting mind, like radar
Mounting higher but veiled and suppressed

Each day living in optimism
Promises fail, marred by pessimism
Causing hardened ambiguity

In a state of provoked mentality
Sentiments bouncing about
In every ace encountered!

Amadou Bh Sey

17 DECEMBER 1998-19 October 2007

MAKE OR BRAKE

Amadou Bh Sey

Relationships that linger
Assurance free
A situation of uncertainty
What's pure is what you have!
What you own
What you control and could actually do
What you see know and believe.

Switch the light on
Or remain in the dark
Making dry substance wet
Turning hot to cold
Living forever in hot beds
Relaxing in waves of doubt

As double dealings rule your minds
Stop pursuing uncertain relations
For every attempt makes things worst
Go in for the good instead of the bad
Stay little or think great
Living small enhances disease

Disease of the mind
Reluctant to heed the call of God
Personalities must be at par with actions
Let's pray for our prayers to be answered
Acting accordingly to God's commandments

Commanding towards good goals
When he needs you to
No doubt you would

Amadou Bh Sey

22 August 1997-19October 2007

WAIT AND SEE!

Valued time rolls on, waiting not hesitant
Procrastinator's brood over moves
The withdrawal syndrome over shadows
That hurts within the silent introvert.

Mean eyes stare, felt by tired views
As faces turn in sudden gaze of envy or hate
Just as they hear my really spoken words
These are valued, so of course I break away
For the mute who hardly speak
Release prophesies!

The language inadequacy that hinders
The fermenting feeling within the cage
Called a chest fencing a scorching heart!

Even the way in which actions are done
Care is taken, caution to any move
The eyes, the hands, the fingers touch
Every minor object about

In a void life of lust and fury!
Lost amidst a nation of culture in veil
The wish to be heard and understood
The confidence thermostatically varies
It rises and falls once from time to time.

Now if you are in mood to go get going
To the ambition to rise and win
To come, to see, to conquer!
Disqualifying all available avenues

Several rolling thoughts that shock
Pulling the veins in a tired mind
All a jumble bundled up into mesh
How I wish to be free from this cauldron!

Amadou Bh Sey

Sunday, 18 November 2007

I NEVER WANTED TO, INDEED

Staying without you is the worst
I ever experienced
God ordained protector of my heart
My total and complete partner

Never I wanted in deep swear
To know another of your kind
But missing your warmth drove me crazy
Insanity covered by loneliness got me trapped and stocked
No longer have I warned should you stay away!

For the more you remain away from me
The deeper, I dive into sin!
And the farther we would be apart
Interim in your absence
Semi-madly I live in expectation.

Searching for what could have been you
Being someone else in peace or war
Amidst threats and warnings
Even those that reserved respect
Now my open enemies!

Foes to me for,
We all target the same goal
All goals of sin I never wanted to aim
So come home now my heart
Too far indeed you are!

AMADOU BH SEY

23 August 1997-Sunday 18 November 2007

LIMITATIONS!

The awareness of what obstructs is now evident
As I am starting to see clearer now!
If only power was to come from the weakened!
Limbs, joints, ligaments, and muscles
Noodles! Pimples of fatigue, pronounced!
The above is within the lecture of an inner voice

Dos and don'ts checks and controls
Warnings all and sundry flow into the saturated mind
Limiting the human, the freedom and the right to survive
To speak, to stroll, to work, to do all
What not, the system has limitations to control men

To none but to immigrants!
Strangers who come into this part of Babylon
The papyrus required, dictates everything!
All accept the ordinance of God!

The shortage of every civilised right
Lives at stake under this umbrella
Of limitations, demarcations, borderlines in all

Only when we sleep that actual liberty comes!
And thus we get entertained by dreams
Most are imaginary until the law acts
Recently the media forecasted on a nearby state
Telling the murder of one of our kind!
Gone forever!
Thus we live on restriction and limitation
A kind of slavery in this modern age
That decrease mentalities to zero level

An insult to all articles and charters ever drafted
For the right of all humankind

AMADOU BH SEY

26 February 2004-18 November 2007

YOUR ABSENCE MY LOVE

Oh darling, my heartaches!
You departed and left me in lust
In sorrow, unrelenting, crazy jeopardy!
You left my mind, body, and soul
In utter dismay!

To you have a similar heart to mine?
How then do you feel?
If you do not,
My side in a joyous moment follows
In another second or so!
Deep sorrow and blankness
My mind remains dark and numb in your absence
My heart unhappy, as it beats slower
I even find living worthless my darling
For without you,
The world becomes void

Some doubt my unusual actions!
For staying late in the vicinity
They claimed that even bachelors
Do resign to bed earlier ha! Ha!
Note! They did encourage our parting!
Knowing not how deep our love is
So going to rest early shocks me more
For I brood all night long
I never got adapted to your absence darling
So please come home now!

AMADOU BH SEY

23 August 1997-**12 April 2012**

WHAT'S YOUR STATUS!

The attire you wear?
The car you drive?
Or those you associate with!
Is it the way you talk?
Or the programs you attend!
All are social depicters of who are
Is it really true of which you really are?
No it is not evident enough
Never judge the books by their covers!
In this class struggle

The job you do and how you relate
The food you eat in the house you live
All and sundry speak
Determining your status quo in this class struggle

The amount of savings in the bank!
What do you do? Where did you get it all and how?
Did they teach you how to look like?
Who decide, the teachers?
The preachers in church alter!
Or the imams in mosque committee members!

Or may most likely the politicians
As they also join the paroles
So who must we believe?
Selfishness only, I condemn
And the class struggle too!

This millennium signals human equality
For all of us shall sadly perish one day
The majority, strive to achieve
The highest class in the so-called status quo!

AMADOU BH SEY

21 December 1997-**12 April 2012**

TRYING!

To make ends meet without means
Lying here and running there
Sometimes a bit of temporary success
At least to smoke a cigar with a cup of coffee!
Eat a plate of rice
Or wear a clumsy jacket

Trying to make it within a concrete jungle
The fever of wanting is haunting indeed
Expecting a lot but earning so meagre
Cry not, Mr Struggler,
For you have no more tears left

So remain in slumber
Appear sad or even act it out
For trying to laugh results in dry cough!
Where laughing could have been a cure
Now may result to a heartbreak
Dry are the wells of emotion
And sympathy is rare!
Thus try and keep up the courage
Just go along and accept your fate!
See what life can provide
Do not lose hope
Just try and keep up the courage
For God is always great!

AMADOU BH SEY

25 November 1999-12 April 2012

NO PAIN BUT A GASH

Even though most parts of society ache
Total ailing state in this, our age of rage
Arms, hearts, joints
Even eyelid lashes wilt!
The ankles of man, waists, and toes also wilt away
A certain shifting sharp ache
Somewhere underneath the stage
Even skulls, the roots of their hair exposed

What a social gash!
A sharp touch of pain
Agonising pain on necks vouch
Now on backs strained for the loads
Causing corns on toes
Society tiptoeing
Not even verifying what's underneath
Of course, the cause we know but gain relief in it
What a dangerous ridicule!

As the shoes we wear hurt
The shirts and trousers tight and hot!
Nothing fits so no pain but a gash
Time to allow nature's pain a pass
Take its right course!
The power to tolerate increase
For when we forget, we decrease

The reel of life goes on and on
The pains felt in hearts momentum got
Assured remedy is constant prayer
Only so shall attain refreshments far

Thus craved for in café stalls
This shifting pain becomes pain no more
As more of it hurts and stays put
So we feel it no more
We are chronic of this pain

AMADOU BH SEY

20 December 1997-12 April 2012

TREATMENT

Please treat me tender
For delicate I am so feeble
I, the heart and soul!
Nothing do I wish for all but well.

So now and then almost all
Treat me without respect!
Even when I spend a life time
Trying to trace what best can be done!

Please do not reject me, my brother
If you knew how much I wish to come!
Closer to you!
You won't be so rigid
So I pray to ALLAH to bring faith!

The light to illuminate thy hearts
Of those whom I deal with
Gradually some are seeing my aim
But several are yet to comprehend.

Or even when they do
Tend not to accept my plight
So futile I remain
Till the chance comes
My way, in this hard time

25 November 1999-Sunday 03 February 2008

WISH

If all wishes had, were to be assured
If we were able to accomplish
Without crying!
Even those who lodge meagre in hunger!
But no! They remain pending and hoping
Like pendulums hoping just to perish!
First and foremost is family stability?
Keep them happy, joyous with faith in their fates.

Dipping thy hands in pockets
Discovering meagre balances
Almighty comes assuring us
As hearts shake in times of crises
For not sure, we remain ever in need
What to or how to assure the doubtful scepticism.

Thus purchase the staple grain
And in tips rations given
Tits and bits of joyous moments even though weak
And attempt to celebrate.

The green herb as mentor together, together
Unite and talk about all and nothing
Please Allah answer to our plight
For peace and progress
Make us earn enough for sustenance

To spend in wisdom at eras of scarcity
No lavish attempt to entertain
As though the providers know not
We are eager just to eat to our full

Allah the merciful the beneficent
Faith in him helps
Plea I to God
Almighty YAARABB
Over turn what might have been!
Distress and sadness to joy and love eternal

Amadou Bh Sey

21 December 1997-Sunday 03 February 2008.

SHOW THE LIGHT OH ALLAH

In the path, before you God
Show the light
Give the power of divinity
Just for us to see the light
Enlighten us to know the hidden secrets
The strength of the faithful sons
The secret code that sets in motion
The good aims harboured in hearts

Just like the sunlight rays at each day brake
The approaching sweet distant swift light of comets
Shooting in the twilight from amidst the universe
Twinkling in the simple vision of humanity
Seen far off above
Seeming not afar but light years away

Just the light, the light flashing at a window
In a dark jungle silent hunters search
In the dark, seeing beckoning lights, of freedom glitter

Now where to shall we move?
Forwards? One step! Semi-optimism
Backwards? Two steps! Staggering pessimism
This doubt pray we, you answer AND help us out
For the power of our minds aren't adequate
Our mental radars too weak
To trace our rescue targets
Just like lost refugees

Thus strangers within ourselves we quest?
To find our real selves in us impossible without you God
Believe that you are nearest to us God
Almighty please push out passion from OUR hearts
Replace that void openness with faith and courage

Amadou Bh Sey

PARIS *accomplished* 20 December 97 VILLEPINTE 16 November 09

INNER VOICE BATTLE

Ability disqualified
In professional undercut
Trying to portray feelings
The void yet to be heard
Condemned or appreciated
This is the peril in consciousness hiding

Within a large complex world of visions
Raging high
But down to zero unknown
For time is yet to bear fruits
All considered fables so far
Yet to be at tune to wishes

Are these mad thoughts?
Or exaggerated hopes
When announce the sound clever
Yet the rhythm is appreciation
Enjoying the feelings, that here is another!
Accomplishments and hangover of the aging

Grey hairs upsetting those in retard
Could the course of nature be avoided?
The really tired computer is the grey coloured matter
The mash of lobes in our brains
Living computers created and time by God!

Amadou Bh Sey

30 May 1998

WHAT HINDERS FREEDOM?

Number one hindrance is the mind
The mental helmet worn by the conscious
As the subconscious supplies the messages
Pushing, exposing, information to active nerves
Activating thus the muscles
Attached to ligaments!
Bones grind and then
Eventual boiling of marrows

Then the world in crises
Who is the world? The people!
In over population
Where does freedom lie?
Feeling independent, then is the answer
This is temporary, for the boredom of other ideas
For thoughts are never exactly synonymous.

Discomfort sometimes in attires!
Rather larger or a bit tighter than expected
Could cut coats to sizes only
When cloth is at hand but not in second hand
That too hinders freedom.

In poverty, filth, and disease
Who could be free?
In starvation and riots
Who could be free?
Not until perfectness descends from heaven!

That force which controls lives on earth
Freeing the minds is the goal
Precious are prayers to help achieve this goal
Without delay!
For any deliberate retard breeds more harm than good.

Amadou Bh Sey

30 May 1998

SELF-DESTRUCTION

Destruction and total annihilation
The ultimate end!
Beings of broken nerves
Alert to be seen or heard
Rarely try to think
Telling the few who listen in rare chances

Doctors confirm.
But do they conform?
The fact that experiments prove
Certain things harm such as herbs!
Thus why easy access to them?
Tobacco smoking is one!
Drinking drunk another!
Sex, too, in prohibition!
Safe sex they say!
Sugar sweet another prudence announced
Several indicated polluting agents
Dangerous radioactivity sums it all up!

Recommending some but several condemned
How then can low calibres survive?
Extremes of opposites compete within,
Our tiny delicate Mother Earth!
Every minute you hope on one of those passers by
Time you start to play your part
To self-revive
And help Mother Earth survive too
Age never increases but reduces life
More and more worthless and weird
As all wears out

Every little thing grows
Alert! Incomplete growth common now
In our day of civilization!
For even larger things degenerate
Still all are and shall be
Until the ultimate end comes
For all will end at one moment
Of a chosen day

Amadou Bh Sey

30 May 1998

THE VOYAGE OF LIFE

Bulls charge and challenge in arenas
As jammed minds hurry
Haunting fear and scepticism
Cuddles up and shy away
Feeling no need to look
Whence around awaiting
The ripeness of time
Departure and search rings in minds
Unavoidable moments of urge
Come up from time to time
But not yet! Minds say

In unfamiliar interactions
Thoughts become blocked
So difficult to portray in speech
May remain dormant, as time is taken
Just to recharge the lost energy
Spent in earlier efforts

Misrepresenting actions
Such as wolves' in sheep's clothing
Just to appear impressive
Hated are those with eyes
That probe gloomy innermost
Magnetic images positively charged
To attract those who love and repel
Deviating from enemies' course
Praying that any other move taken
Convinces to max any being
In whatever situation appreciated
So difficult a task but not impossible

Any aim can be achieved
So long there is life
Who could provide the humour?
To love and embrace even open enemies!

Amadou Bh Sey

29 May 1998

AS I ARRIVED

All is yet to come yonder that horizon
The wealth craved for, in this region
The love craved for, even in caves
The knowledge craved for in rates so high
These are but void.

Open large highways cars flow
Long vehicles, slide, and trucks too throw
Light, amidst glittering Florence
Million pedestrians, striving for heights!

Flyovers hovering over busy heads
Multiple surging, rushing crowds thread
Multi-coloured dresses of people and lights
Maintenance, crumbling structures
Slogans decorating open walls, beside pavements
Many of my kind in substandard tight homes

On the other side as TV show
Indeed is hidden glamour but
Woe be tide the windows of the world we seek
Every single day another experience

The attractive dames, swiftly walking
Mute and looking straight ahead
Swift walkers and buyers shop too
Restaurants serving the class!
Those who could afford the franc
Survive! With the F you are master

Amadou Bh Sey

03 June 1998

SATURATION

In blockage of raging thoughts, rotating in a cage
Undeniably confusing actions on the stage of supposed life
Inability to identify the melodrama
Destination in question, occupation mysteriously in gloom, a claim

So indoors, lack of endurance
The cause or the effort to recapitulate
So weakened not enhanced
Though active in the creativity of letters
This brain seems drained of reality in fetters
Exhausted, thus couldn't harbour strains at hand

Life is meant to be free
Or curtailed short at once
Scarce alternatives causing revolving fear within
Whence the motive rises, readiness is eminent
Sure millions of ideas and suggestions flow in
But implementation in doubt,
As words and sound are mere sound and air.

Just about tile to get on
But mental dictates deny
If was a stage, already set and arranged
All in motion now but this body in chains of sorrow
The morrow that freedom comes never seems to arrive
Flexing the ever ready muscles
Within a sea of ambitions
No opportunity yet to exercise this excess energy

All the imagination of the possible
The possibilities are but a question
Yet so abundant but hard to attain
Exploit what's on display therefore man
Wits get weakened
In pondering over dead matters
A stable heart equals a tranquil mind
Reciprocally they assure success if balanced
So when would the required readiness arrive?

Amadou Bh Sey

27 June 1997

LINGERING HOPE IN SOLITUDE

Life oozing along awaiting none,
All aspects in extremity
A mass of substandard assimilated humans,
The fading of faith in hearts, that once surged in virtue.
For faith breeds virtue
But freethinking, unguarded, hardens the heart!
Like a baked brick of kaolinite mineral.

Soothsayers posing as spiritual supreme ministers
Struggling in the greed for recognition and fame
In expensive dresses, the need for money, too, worsens!
Gambling out for success abed

The dream for higher heights in every being
The adverts that trigger the cords of the poor!
For they see, that's the end
Nothing to purchase of what's shown
The capitalists' wealth, their cars, and abundant food
Are but a passing dream in life

No hearts for the strange, within the fried cages of their ribs!
Just robots' as machine utility dictates
A victim of language inadequacy dies mute,
For no one listens if you express in another.

Isolation is a merit
But at least a TVs keeps company
Awaiting a call to set you free, alive on again
Just after a long day of silence

Amadou Bh Sey

3 June 1998

VIEW OF HILL TOP RUE PIAT PARIS FRANCE

Vivid glancing I sight the crappers
Timidly I saw, though in doubt
What they hold in the distance
Yonder vents for monoxide ooze

Western horizon brightening
As the sun sets golden glow
Above the story buildings
Appearing as tall, dead, cut outs of art

So unrealistic for doubt in their content
Down looking not so low,
Enough, do they spell out
Enough, gathered when even fools talk!

Hearing them speak makes me sick, stupid
Confusingly narrating anyhow,
Endless and baseless
Do you comprehend the dieting world?
Dancing and drinking to hell headed

Surprising first impression
Is this the world we dream of?
Not enough, for yet more to come!
Egos crave, moving into graves
Too much for a 'Johnny just coming'
Be ready, oh men and women in the hustling Diaspora!
To face your fates with your faith!

Amadou Bh Sey

3 MAY 1998

'MOTIVE' IN PARIS

To move to where!
I wondered round
Not enough fuel
To even taste!
Lack of tempo and
The zeal that propels so
Decelerating in dull moods!

Disparity and dismay in my ever rolling thoughts
For even abed I think deep
Is this my destiny?
An accident of nature!

The pendulum system persists
No resistance as the urge pulls
Indeed move or even a flicker of hope
Could do for those locked in the dark
To automate my weakened engine

Blaming oneself isn't virtue
For a vicious conscience comes about
And lingers for years unaided
So absurd and odd I live
A stranger, always!

Opinions pushed and ideas given
But none and never could
Solutions come in time
Yes! Good God comes in time to aid the needy
When and how? He alone likes.

Amadou Bh Sey

5 June 1998

DEDICATED FRIENDSHIP

Although still on commencement
We seem to have cemented
Our fragile hearts in a pair, minds on set
Our thought in unison

Your kindness bubbles
Given chance may double
Could I measure up?
For only praises I have in response

As though years long we saw
Yet just for countable days sure
Nothing I could think of could suffice*
To balance or match up your device

So now atom of few words in response
For yet have to recover from my shock
Of years on in suffering and bondage
So thanks my friend!

Let's all pray to the one whom!
All praises belong to God!
For only He can enhance
And on him I bestow all hope!

Amadou Bh Sey

27 April 1998

IN A COCOON IN PARIS

Within it we wriggle and attempt to jiggle,
But mostly circumstances evade
When we went to wiggle out
As our wishes wait unsolved!

Couldn't ever germinate arid
Dormant until time comes ripe!
The kinetic strive to survive goes on
The octopus that captures victims

Tentacles surrounding not only their brains but also their actions too
Thus keep on shaking for sake of freedom!
To live out of this cells of thought
Pessimism regarding worthwhile actions

Scepticism kills! Valuable beings;
For doubts they dwell, never assured
Till at the brink of life, after several deaths
Cajoled only after the sip of the poison on sale!
As cups are gulped
Viewing drunkards forming circles around

Shaking hands of hags
Hugs revealed unrealistic illusions
In chats that develop into conversations.

These cocoons are never open
Have to dig out of their invisibility
Factually they aren't invulnerable
So in faith, they accept their fate.

Thus the living beings within these cocoons,
Are but rather too sensitive to cope
Except unavoidable circumstances
Trying to run away
But not from their innermost

Amadou Bh Sey

Tuesday 11 August 1998

RAGING NERVES IN PARIS

Execute evil and its cause and source
Somewhere!
Every hidden or exposed corner,
Are victims of vices?
More harmful is the fear of the glares
Where gossips disappear and evaporate in to vain

Just plunge ahead and venture
But be sure to comprehend
Where shall the right urge emerge?
That which would animate vigils in slumber

Enthusiastic minds, rocking
Imaging under surveillance
Shaking consciences
What shall thus assure security?

Void, vainness, emptiness, all machinating!
A voice says you are innocent
So go ahead high!
Run your way or drill deep down.

These are mixed feelings
How I wish to obtain a calm listener!
Adoring, simple, quiet natural and calm
Or shall so, remain a victim of my rolling conscience!
Then gather I, enough courage to charge!

Amadou Bh Sey

INSIDE THE BOX (TV) IN PARIS

Thanks and praises to jiljalali
Who gave us ears in his power!
Without which no one would have heard
Not even your essence!
Entertainer, educator, informer

Fills the gaps, in eras of loneliness
Worthy of your cost, your inventor!
Substitute, in the absence of lovers' whispers
When acquaintances aren't around

Informers of both, sad and happy news
From the north, east, south, and west
Electrical voice crack, sharp and audible!
Without a single lip neither a tongue!

Sometimes so portable
When large at one place steady
Without you a null world of void and silence
Telling us about astronauts!

Even words of faith you sermon
Linking us with everyone else
When on, life is worthy of living and coloured
Valued even in the dark
No condition for message revolves

Amadou Bh Sey

20 April, 1998

THE FEAR OF CHANGE

The evil doer's tired naked eyes
Haphazardly wink as they scrutinize
Deliberately repeating jeopardy
As sobered ones comprehend and bear the pain

Sobered brains assume to know ways out
Suggesting possible outlets
Seeming sure of what they preach
To motivate the badly needed change

It is a challenge to face change
'To take the bull by its horns'
Halt all that stimulates exhausted limbs
A whirling pool of indecision,
Amidst, every change!

All wits are animated
Resulting into ultimate failures
As time burns out
A total disintegration!
Of gathered courage enough for the Titanic!

A centre of all assurance
Is a purified mind
Free from force and fashion
Without any urge
In disorder this final decision gets defused

All then jumble into an endless quest of doubt
Redoubling flowing thoughts
Those jam up and get stuck!
These coexist in a rotten growth
Thus a recycle of fear of change is born!

Amadou Bh Sey

20 December 1997

THE QUITTING LIMBO

Habits learnt early in the prime,
A permanent stain as if natural
In this forms Mr Danger beckoner
To nullify beautiful gifts of nature once had
Such as the air we breathe

Now you, in the hook of smoke
Cross that dangling bridge
Stretch thy minds' reserved power
Not to wait for the receding tomorrows
Those morrows shall never come!
Trust in the original form to restore

Whence done shall never be undone
A dream comes true
Resume good actions Mr Addict!
For when carried out they wouldn't hide
For the virtue of being natural
Is beauty that shines!

But not to remain in total shatter!
Or a random thought of peril
So never forget that God ordains
No matter what we wish
His will is final and always sure.

Amadou Bh Sey

21 December 1997

INTERNAL 'PEACE' TRANQUILITY

This, periodical inner liberty
Try to communicate my innermost feelings
To the One and Only ONE God
In whom doubt not thee, in His existence
The eternal kingdom of the Supreme!

Feel Him in and all around you total,
Though seeing Him not, He sees thy heart
Noticing your thoughts and aiding
Helping in the realization of dreams
Persistently, I pray to remain worshipping Him

Wholly to the Holy
Submitting in bows, in honesty, earnestly
His manifestations so profoundly distinct
For the faithful and wise
Vast has He shown His omnipotence
The power guiding those blindfolded.

Adequately providing for all
His 'Rahmanity'—mercifully embrace
All and sundry in this world and
The hereafter in His 'Rahimity'
Pray I, the minds in a storm to settle calm.

Feeling Him, offers irrefutable tranquillity
As He removes the sin and guilt of repentance
Beg for His pardon
And forgive He Will
Praise the praiseworthy
The king of kings!
Crave to be purified in His Holiness.

Amadou Bh Sey

May 29 1998

CRAVING

Rage gravity pulling
Craving for love wishing
Still none existent
Night and day thinking and waiting
Even my image demonstrates.

This wish hangs around
As if a rope tied my neck
The hunger of love drains my heart
Every night so long, alone!

Thus loneliness rules
Thoughts feed my weakened passion
Every little action calculated
Just to qualify a passage.

As so many do
I also indeed require
To satisfy a natural call
To get accomplished;

At least for one
A special unique dame
Maternally on the alert
To be a recipient of my dreams
Until that occurs, nights shall remain long
Cold and lonely in dismay

Amadou Bh Sey

13 October 1998

CAUTION

Surprising merits could be chances too
Beyond expectations!
Interact, receive, and chat
In every conference of humans

Bless the slightest virtue
And smile to even vice, heals evil
Not to mimic twitches or killing spirits
But broadly switched and radiating joy

Stand firm on thy feet
Thread gently on nature's mat
Spread your wings
For all creation and creatures
Never usurp a valued privilege.

Exploit not your fellow man
See beyond racial boundaries
Penetrate the walls of class
Associate and wish all success
Prosperity and everlasting joy

Keep cool and ride smooth
Give way to passers-by in hurry
Hurry not!
For towards reaching the end you may fall!

Amadou Bh Sey

29 May 1998

VOID FREEDOM

Get checked and feel watched
Never abuse leisure at hand
Freedom becomes passion in usurp
Realizing the value of time

The value of which roles on
Awaiting no hesitant around
In our hard times constant
So use the free relax time well

Void so void without the warmth
The worth of which we all search out
Look for one to keep us warm
No more, waste of this freedom

Filled with thoughts
Rushing ideas within
Thus to apply these concepts
My hands and mouth hang, as I watch

But to writ I must
To vent out the hot thoughts
Making me a writer
Spouting out reeling thoughts
Worth so much to do with my time
No more than its source
Thus void is freedom
Till used well to serve all.

Amadou Bh Sey

25 May 98-2 December 1998

THIS CHILD I CALL 'G'

Call him an adolescent of void experience
Young head of early twenties
Onset welcome, degenerated to insults
For me as a stranger with this child
I call G

Rolling in lectures of the incomprehensible
Venturing into metro burrows in Paris
With this child I call G
Running back home to wash plates
Broken-hearted I still remain
With this child I call G

With the face of a demon
Chuckling up teeth,
That ride on each other
Rushing about in the tiny ghetto
Still with this child I call G
In which he claims to be king of kings

Now and then dispersing the bric-a-brac
That was already in disorder!
Every action of this child I call G is mal
Too rude to recognize respect and discipline

He spoke only the language of this land, France
Franco minded is this child I call G
Oriented only to walk about
Acting in a state of delirium
So far a slight change came

After this child call G started to learn
Good manners
A visit to where we all belong
Oh Africa! My motherland

                                        Amadou BH Sey

17 May 1998

TRUST NOT WHAT THEY SAY

A bunch of lies and promises swiftly fade
When got carried by mere words
As they smile and act as if kind!
But no! I deny!
No more trust on what I hear
Until I could see its effects;

No matter how many words uttered
What I believe is what's done
Time told, is telling now
Time will then tell
And shall always tell in the end
As the demands based on hopes vanish!
So many shocks!
Caused by failed promises
So role on as if nothing was said.

I do live along though
Still penetrating the impermeable
As boulders of speeches descend
From mouths releasing words of doubt
Dumbfounded I just shut up
But so sensitive, remain my eyes and ears.

In trickles some become generous
As few tips drop in
Bigger are the chances
For every discovery is valued

Amadou Bh Sey

25 May, 1998

THE QUEST

Rocking in an imaginary little boat
All in scepticism doubting and idling
As my will get dampened
And my craving heart pump harder

Descending or climbing the hill of Rue Piat in Paris
Climbing the steps of this ever valued first floor
With the keys in my pocket
As my mind dictates what I daren't attempt
Where to go?
What to do?
What to say or deny?

This state of dilemma tires me
My freedom in question
Hoping to achieve one day
The imagined alter in my mind's eye

Nothing beyond what time and circumstances can provide
When around I rush into the cave
As I try to look closer it recedes
Are there any more opportunities?
Of course I believe there are
Somewhere around the corners I search

The light of love and virtue
Is all I crave for?
With wisdom and prudence as my tools
And now is the dawn of my alter
Here or yonder, it shines beckoning
I hope it shall soon be noon at home?

Amadou Bh Sey

25 May 1998

OH GOD WHICH LOVE?

I need the love of God
He is the everlasting and always around
He is in company of those in destitute

Yes, within all cores god is found
All minds, all hearts contain Him
All peripheries, covered by His mercy

Revolving around are other loves
I value only one love
The love of the almighty and merciful

Grow in it you are assured
No comparison to other loves
For all, are but fallacies
That shall one day fade away

So I still search for this love
From his creations
But this love is pain
So I pray to contain the pain of divine love
And I pray not to be prey for false lovers
Thus enjoy here and the hereafter

Amadou Bh Sey

THE DESIRE

To have one my mind thinks
A free one, only for me alone, at link
But for one I remain true
And only when I encounter you,
Shall I realize life is worth living!

The need to catch
My image as bait so large
The thoughts and desires interwoven
As suggestions flow to prove

I run after one, up a shelter
Now one runs after me to delta
To my awareness this one shall prop
Soon another may emerge from the lot

All, as I wish for one
The one I want
And now one craves for me, but ranked high
So thus God I pray
That you intervene in my sways
Bring the decision aloof
Make both into reality, through
For I for one needs my lord's wisdom
To survive in the concrete jungle

Amadou Bh Sey

JEALOUSY!

Is it malice?
Call it antagonism
Or hidden hatred

Is it an obstacle?
Or a signal of hindrance to progress
Expression of boiling fury
Hating, furious faces, regard
Any acceleration of rising suns

Attacking of scorn
Jealousy is a frustrating chronic itch
Fetched in time to harm
Releasing and shining on bony faces
Greedily groping at all threats

Threatening the slightest signs of hope shown
Accepting such pushes just to become number one!
Bearing to be labelled a stooge
A good for nothing guy

Gathered over years of pain
So justified is to make it
The slogan of the foreigner
Enemy you stand! Mr Jealous man
Challenges you face too amongst those too
Those of your creed know not love

Amadou Bh Sey

ANOTHER DAY IN LIMBO

With my heartily partner in bed
After all caressing into vain
Just because fear of being heard
My our hosts who just sneak to hear

Suspicious and grudging neighbours
In robes of hypocrisy
Oh, another day and night in limbo
Helpless we cancelled
What could have been a sweet love session!

As I heaved and turned away
As my darling wondered
Rolling in bed in doubt and thirst
Thus we prayed to god
To give us a home
And total autonomy.

As we seem so in need
As hustlers we bear
Dead we were of fear to be heard
For simple reason being shy
So help us God
We need a private home
In peace and love

Amadou Bh Sey

28 July 2001 5 a.m.

HOW I WISH

Oh, how I wish to acquire that inner pulse of peace!
Even though yet to achieve my ultimate goal I plead
Oh, how I wish to have a constant mental smile
All as I rove and trance along
The tough, rough, challenging rues of Paris

To maintain an everlasting
Ever flourishing virtue an undying love
That which would keep me smiling
Day in day out above
Oh, how I wish my face spells welcome, bearing
Featuring radiance, a smiling heart reforming

Oh, how I wish to reply in cordiality
To do away with a constantly burning heart, radicalism
Replacing it with an overflowing constant embrace
That even fools could read
Not to erase, no haste

Oh, how I wish to demonstrate enough taste
An image of acceptance, regardless of all race or creed
No borderline no restrictions, to all good thoughts welcome
To speak out words of joy, to listeners worth and satisfaction

How I wish to joke and laugh and be open
Without calculating, in a relaxed mind
To be jovial at all moments about and aloud
Where all around would enjoy, reciprocally
And those away and far miss, virtually

How I wish to pray too at times of deep depress!
Dream beautifully, reflect, and thus act positively, through
All conditions, a wish, oh! How I wish not to be too sensitive
Just live moderate, and no threats, reflective, and optimized
Oh, how I wish to have confidence, totally
And indeed finally get convinced and satisfied
What does life has to offer?
But would timidity allow?
So as my thoughts roll on
Whirling around inside out
So the out let is my pen on paper
My friend and my mind
Remains a fountain to spout
Ideas are still deep down to be shared
Thanks to all those who read me,
And my regards to all who care!

Amadou Bh Sey

17 October 1998

AUTHOR'S BIOGRAPHY

Amadou Bh Sey

I was born in a village, in one of the former British colonies in the West coast of Africa. This country gained its independence on 18 February 1965. In 1975, I passed my common entrance examination, with scholarship. I left my native village for the first time to attain high school education at the only government boarding school. Armitage high school and is where I had my first inspiration to write a poem in 1978. I read this poem to the whole school at the assembly hall, during a Saturday night impromptu concert. In Armitage, I acquired a lot of aspiration and experience, which haunted and influenced my life onwards.

After high school, I started teaching as an untrained teacher, the following subjects: History and civics or government. This was from 1980 to 1982 at the capital city, Banjul junior secondary technical school. I was eventually transferred to Saint Augustine's junior secondary school in September 1982 to July 1983.

Then I joined Action Aid, a UK-based NGO for developing countries. I continued teaching in CLCs equivalent to primary schools called 'community learning centres' at Madina-sasita primary school and Sitahuma primary school from October 1983 to July 1987.

By merit of hard work and competence, I was promoted to the status of a headmaster and transferred to Naode primary school; I got married in 1988, and my wife joined me at Naode in 1989. I was transferred to Gunjur Kuta in 1990 March. My first child, a boy, was born on 20 August 1990. Alternately, I obtained a qualified, experienced teacher certificate, following six years of in-service training course. This course was financed, conducted, and tutored by the ministry of education and the participation of, the teachers' union, member of the EI, *education international*. This was in collaboration with The Bunumbu university college, Sierra-Leon. The course was monitored by The New Castle University in the UK. Consequently, I returned to the ministry of education at the end of my service with Action Aid

International. I was transferred to Bansang primary school from 1991 to 1993. Finally, before going to France to further my studies on scholarship, I was posted to Gunjur junior secondary school in the western division of my country. From September 1993 to March 1998, the year I came to France.

In France, I had two intensive training courses in French called *FLE (francais langue etrangere)* with FIDE *formation, l'insertion, development ET l'education* from 1999 to 2001. Consequently, I was admitted to continue on a bilingual course of English and French with GRETA, at where I attained a professional certificate in translation, public relations, and communication from 2001 to 2003.

Thus with these qualifications, I opted to work in France. For Railrest Company, a high speed train service with Thalys international company, since August 2003 to date. I have a past rich and cultured experience of eighteen years of teaching, in Africa and nine years of work with Railrest. I specialize in check-in, boarding ticket control, information, and orientation of passengers, at Gard du Nord train station, Paris; departures of international passengers heading to Brussels, Amsterdam in Holland, and Düsseldorf in Germany.

Whenever I am not at work or out with my family, I keep on writing. My hobbies are cycling, walking, reading, writing, music, watching movies, and of course the NEWS on TV. Being a pious and humble person I spend hours each day in meditation and prayers. I have five children. Three boys and two girls, they are all presently at school-going age. I have been on active service, both in Africa and Europe. This makes me a highly field experienced person. The poems of diverse visions, *heritage, in Africa* from my cradle to 1998, I now live in *the Diaspora in France*. My family and I have been granted French citizenship since 2008.

Being a graduate from a university without walls, in the republic of letters, where the libraries and faculties are the people and their lives. I have lived to learn as I try to attain by doctorate degree, of learning how to learn, thus telling the story by writing poetry, for now. From the actions, thoughts, and deeds of my characters, I continue to learn how to learn. *My notion of education is from womb to tomb.*

Amadou Bh Sey